W9-ACP-542

DEUTERONOMY AND TRADITION

DEUTERONOMY AND TRADITION

by E. W. NICHOLSON

PHILADELPHIA
FORTRESS PRESS

American Edition
first published 1967 by
Fortress Press, Philadelphia

Library of Congress Catalog Card Number 67-22200

5563D67 Printed in U.S.A. 1-291

To My Mother
In Piam Memoriam

PREFACE

This book has its basis in a thesis entitled *Literary and Historical Problems in the Book of Deuteronomy* which was submitted to the Faculty of Arts in the University of Glasgow for the degree of Ph.D. in 1964. Since completing this thesis I have had the opportunity of reading further and more recent works which deal directly with or impinge upon the study of Deuteronomy. As a result of this many of the conclusions and ideas expressed in the thesis have been changed or modified in preparing this work.

I wish to express my gratitude to my supervisor in Glasgow University, Professor C. J. Mullo Weir, and his colleagues Professor J. Mauchline and Dr William McKane for their generous help and guidance during my period as a research student. My thanks are also due to Professor J. Weingreen who has given freely of his time and advice and whose interest in this work has been a constant encouragement to me. I am especially indebted to Professor G. W. Anderson for reading through the manuscript and making many helpful suggestions which have contributed significantly to this book. To all these scholars I am greatly indebted. What merit this book may have is due largely to their interest and guidance whilst its weaknesses and faults must be attributed to me alone. I wish also to thank my friend Mr John Neill who has performed the tedious task of checking the many references contained in the manuscript. Finally, a special word of thanks is due to my wife whose forbearance and patience enabled me to devote more time to this work than would otherwise have been possible.

Biblical quotations throughout this study are from the Revised Standard Version with the exception of Chapter II where it has been necessary to quote from the Revised Version for the purposes of illustrating the change from the second person singular form of address to the second person plural which is discussed in this chapter.

I dedicate this little book to the memory of my mother who first read to me the words of the Bible and who herself lived in its light and died in its hope.

Trinity College, Dublin
March 1966

E. W. NICHOLSON

CONTENTS

INTRODUCTION

The problem with which we are concerned in this short study is that of the origin of the book of Deuteronomy and the circles responsible for its composition. This problem is among the most controversial in Old Testament studies. At one time or another almost every period in Israel's history from Moses to the post-exilic period has been advanced as the age in which the book was composed, whilst its authorship has been ascribed variously to Moses himself, Samuel or, less specifically, to prophetic, priestly and other circles. As to origin, it has been associated with such sanctuaries as Jerusalem, Shechem and Bethel or, less precisely, to northern Israel or Judah.

From the point of view of literary criticism it has been widely agreed that the book was composed in the seventh century B.C. The great literary critical school of the last century regarded it as having originated among people who were heirs of the ethical teaching of the eighth-century prophets who were generally held by this school to have been the innovators and source of the high ethical and spiritual qualities in the Old Testament. As a seventh-century literary creation reflecting the teaching of these prophets, Deuteronomy was accorded a position late in the evolutionary process which led, in Wellhausen's thought, from the primitive religion of the Patriarchs through the henotheism of later times to the exalted monotheism of Deutero-Isaiah and the literature of the exilic and post-exilic period.

Today such a view would find few supporters. Quite apart from an unwillingness to impose upon the religion of the Old Testament any such evolutionary pattern as that advocated by Wellhausen and his contemporaries, the advent of form-criticism and the traditio-historical investigation of the literature of the Old Testament has made it quite clear that the actual books in it are but the end products of a long history of the traditions which they embody. Thus the prophetic literature is now commonly regarded as being the final product of the long transmission of the oracles of the prophets by their circles of disciples, whilst the documents which literary criticism isolated in the Pentateuch—J, E, D, P, H—are themselves regarded as being the written deposit of much older traditions. For the book of Deuteronomy, with which we are particularly concerned, this has meant that although it was actually composed at a relatively late date in Israel's history—almost certainly, as older scholars suggested, in the seventh century B.C.—the traditions upon which it is based are very much older. Hence the problem of the origin of Deuteronomy becomes a study in the history of the traditions which it embodies. Nor is it any longer possible to see with scholars of a former generation Deuteronomy's high ethical and humanitarian qualities as reflecting the teaching of the eighth-century prophets, for recent research has made it clear that these prophets cannot be regarded as the innovators of ethics into Israel's religion. It is now apparent in fact that they themselves were heirs of a long and deeply embedded morality which points for its origins to the covenant which from the beginning of her history defined Israel's relationship with Yahweh.

The Old Testament has provided us with a key position from which we can begin our investigation. In 2 Kings xxii–xxiii it is recorded that in the reign of Josiah in the last years of the seventh century a 'book of the law' was found in the Temple in Jerusalem. It has been widely, though by no means universally, agreed that this book was the book of Deuteronomy at least in its original form. Our first task will be therefore to examine this view. If it can be substantiated it will supply us with two vital points for our investigation, for it will establish that the book was in existence by the late seventh century and that its promulgation was associated with the Jerusalem Temple. The consideration of this problem will be followed by a discussion of the contents of that book, that is, the parts of the present book of Deuteronomy which belonged to it. This is necessitated by the fact that the book in its present form displays evidence of a long literary growth, which clearly raises the possibility that later hands have inserted notions which were not held by the authors of the original book and which may on this account mislead us in our investigation of the provenance of the book. We shall then attempt to determine the nature of Deuteronomy from the point of view of the traditions upon which it is based and to isolate its distinctive ideas and characteristics. This will lead us directly to a consideration of where and amongst what circles such traditions and ideas had their origin and home. The solution of this problem will provide us with a possible solution as to the provenance and authorship of the book.

CHAPTER I

DEUTERONOMY AND JOSIAH'S REFORMATION[1]

ONE of the first major strides taken in the history of the scientific study of the Old Testament was W. M. L. De Wette's thesis that the 'book of the law' which was found in the Temple in Jerusalem in the eighteenth year of Josiah's reign (2 Kings xxii–xxiii) was substantially the book of Deuteronomy. Since De Wette's *Dissertatio Critica*[2] in 1805 this equation of Josiah's law book with the whole or, as is more usual, part of Deuteronomy[3] has become virtually the cornerstone of Pentateuchal criticism. In spite of the dissent of a number of scholars,[4] the majority of critics accepted the theory that Deuteronomy was written during the seventh century B.C., whether under Hezekiah or Manasseh or Josiah they were not agreed, and that it was placed in the Temple by its authors and discovered there in

[1] Part of this chapter originally appeared as an article in *TGUOS* 20 (1963–64), pp. 77–84. I am grateful to the editor, Professor C. J. Mullo Weir, for permission to reprint some of it here.

[2] His doctoral thesis *Dissertatio critica, qua Deuteronomium a prioribus Pentateuchi libris diversum, alius cuiusdam recentioris auctoris opus esse monstratur* (1805) reprinted in his *Opuscula* (Berlin, 1833). Cf. his *Beiträge zur Einleitung in das A.T.*, vol. I (1806). The view that Josiah's law book was Deuteronomy had already been suggested by some of the early fathers, notably Athanasius, Jerome, Chrysostom and Procopius of Gaza, and at a later time by Hobbes and Lessing. Cf. E. Nestle, 'Das Deuteronomium und II Könige xxii', *ZAW* 22 (1902), pp. 170–171, 312–313; J. Hempel, 'Chronik', *ZAW* 51 (1933) p. 299 n. 1; H. H. Rowley, 'The Prophet Jeremiah and the Book of Deuteronomy', now in his *From Moses to Qumran* (London, 1963), p. 194 n. 2.

[3] The majority of those who accepted De Wette's theory were agreed that not all of the present book of Deuteronomy lay before Josiah. On this problem see Chapter II below.

[4] The traditional Mosaic authorship of Deuteronomy and the rest of the Pentateuch was vigorously defended by a number of commentators, notably by E. W. Hengstenberg, H. A. C. Hävernick, and C. F. Keil. At the other extreme a group of nineteenth-century scholars dated the composition of Deuteronomy as late as the exilic or post-exilic period. Cf. C. W. P. Gramberg, *Kritische Geschichte der Religionsideen des A.T.*, vol. I (1829), pp. 153f., 305f.; W. Vatke, *Die Religion des A.T. nach den kanonischen Büchern* (1835), pp. 504f.; L. Seinecke, *Geschichte des Volkes Israel*, vol. I (1876), p. 386, vol. II (1884), pp. 1–20; E. Havet, *Le Christianisme et ses Origines*, vol. III (1878), p. 8; G. d'Eichthal, *Mélanges de Critique Biblique* (1886), pp. 81ff.; M. Vernes, *Une Nouvelle Hypothèse sur la Composition du Deutéronome* (1887); idem, *Précis d'Histoire Juive* (1889), pp. 468ff.; L. Horst, 'Etudes sur le Deutéronome', *RHR* 16 (1887), pp. 28–65; 17 (1888), pp. 1–22; 18 (1888), pp. 320–334; 23 (1891), pp. 184–200; 27 (1893), pp. 119–176; E. Day, 'The Promulgation of Deuteronomy', *JBL* 21 (1902), pp. 197–213; S. A. Fries, *Die Gesetzschrift des Königs Josia* (1903).

621 B.C. to become the basis of a sweeping reformation carried out by Josiah.[1] This theory is so well known that only a short résumé of it need be given here.[2]

In 2 Kings xxii–xxiii[3] we are told that in the eighteenth year of king Josiah's reign some repairs were being carried out in the Temple (xxii. 3f.) and that the king sent the scribe Shaphan to Hilkiah, the high priest, with certain instructions concerning the financing of the repair work. Hilkiah gave Shaphan a 'book of the law' which he had found in the Temple. The scribe read it and in his turn brought it to the king (xxii. 8f.). On hearing its contents, Josiah was greatly alarmed and sent a deputation to the prophetess Huldah to consult the oracle of Yahweh concerning the threats which the book evidently contained (xxii. 10f.). Huldah replied pronouncing doom upon the people and land because of their apostasy and idolatry (xxii. 15–17) but promising Josiah himself that he would not witness the coming disaster because of his penitent and humble reaction to the contents of the newly discovered book (xxii. 18–20). The king then convoked an assembly of the people and there followed a covenant ceremony in which the king and people pledged themselves 'to perform the words of this covenant that were written in this book' (xxiii. 1–3). Following this a reformation was inaugurated to implement the demands of the law book (xxiii. 4f.).[4] All the cult objects pertaining to the worship of Baal and Asherah and the 'host of heaven' were removed from the Temple and burned outside the city in the Kidron valley (xxiii. 4). At the same time the paraphernalia of the Assyrian Shamash cult was destroyed (xxiii. 11). The Phoenician, Moabite and Ammonite cult centres which Solomon is said to have built south-east of Jerusalem (1 Kings xi. 5, 7) were destroyed (xxiii. 13). Idolatrous priests who had been installed at shrines throughout Judah were deposed (xxiii. 5).[5] Various obnoxious practices such as cult prostitution (xxiii. 7), the Molech cult with its

[1] For a complete bibliography see A. R. Siebens, *L'Origine du Code Deutéronomique* (Paris 1929), pp. 23–24.

[2] The classical statement of this theory can be found in such works as S. R. Driver's *Deuteronomy* (*ICC*[3], Edinburgh, 1902), and his *Introduction to the Literature of the O.T.* (9th edit., Edinburgh, 1913). A. R. Siebens' work referred to in the previous footnote offers an excellent survey of the debate on Deuteronomy during the earlier part of this century.

[3] The Chronicler's account (2 Chron. xxxiv–xxxv) is quite different from that in Kings and will be dealt with at a later stage in our discussion.

[4] The narrative clearly implies that the law book motivated the reformation in spite of Pedersen's remark (*Israel: Its Life and Culture III–IV*, Copenhagen 1940, p. 579) that 'it is not expressly stated that the law book caused the reform'.

[5] On the interpretation of כמרים as 'eunuch priests' see W. F. Albright, *From the Stone Age to Christianity*[2] (Baltimore, 1946), pp. 178, 325 n. 46.

human sacrifices (xxiii. 10), and demon cults (xxiii. 8b)[1] were rooted out. Pagan cults and altars innovated by Ahaz and Manasseh were destroyed (xxiii. 12). In addition, and perhaps most significant of all, the Yahweh sanctuaries throughout all Judah were destroyed and their priests brought up to Jerusalem where cultic worship was henceforth to be centralized (xxiii. 8a, 9). The reformation was also extended to northern Israel where the shrine at Bethel was evidently singled out for particularly severe treatment (xxiii. 15f).

The theory of De Wette and his successors is based upon the belief that a law book of such manifest importance could not have been lost and that it must therefore now form part of the Old Testament and, more specifically, of the legal sections of the Pentateuch. It was then observed that there are striking parallels between the reform measures carried out by Josiah and the demands of Deuteronomy. The king's enactments can be explained for the most part by Deuteronomy and some of them, especially the abolition of the Yahweh high places and the centralization of the cult, only by it. This can readily be appreciated from the following table:[2]

2 Kings xxiii	Deuteronomy
Abolition of the Asherim *vv.* 4, 6, 7, 14	vii. 5; xii. 3; xvi. 21.
The host of heaven *vv.* 4, 5	xvii. 3.
Destruction of the 'pillars' *v.* 14	vii. 5; xii. 3; etc.
Heathen high places *v.* 13	vii. 5; xii. 2f.; etc.
Sun and moon worship *vv.* 5, 11	xvii. 3.
Sacred prostitution *v.* 7	xxiii. 18 (EVV 17)
Molech cult *v.* 10	xii. 31; xviii. 10.
Foreign gods, etc. *v.* 13	xii; xiii.
Necromancy *v.* 24	xviii. 11.
Passover celebrated in Jerusalem, i.e. centralized Passover *vv.* 21–23	xvi. 1–8.

Hence it was concluded that Josiah's law book is to be identified with Deuteronomy at least in its original form, the so-called *Urdeuteronomium*. This theory is of cardinal importance for several reasons. In the first place, it clearly fixes the *terminus ad quem* for the composition of Deuteronomy in 621 B.C. and is therefore of great significance

[1] MT reads הַשְּׁעָרִים 'gates'. The reading 'demon' or 'satyr' is obtained by a slight change in the pointing—הַשְּׂעִרִים. Cf. J. A. Montgomery and H. S. Gehman, *Kings* (*ICC*, Edinburgh, 1951), in loc.

[2] For a complete list of parallels see L. B. Paton, 'The Case for the Post-exilic Dating of Deuteronomy', *JBL* 47 (1928), pp. 325f.

in the discussion of the period in which the book originated. Secondly, it associates the promulgation of the book with the Jerusalem Temple and draws a direct connection between its demands and the reform measures carried out by Josiah. It is on this account of importance in the discussion of the provenance of Deuteronomy.

The theory has not, however, gone unchallenged. It was, as we have noted, rejected by a strong body of nineteenth-century scholars, the so-called Gramberg school,[1] who advanced the theory of an exilic or post-exilic date for the origin of Deuteronomy and in so doing denied that it could have been Josiah's law book.[2] This view has persisted and has been advocated in this century by scholars such as Hölscher, Kennett, Horst, Cook and Pedersen.[3] Since it is currently favoured by several scholars[4] it is necessary to examine it briefly here.[5]

The debate has centred chiefly on the problem of the extent to which the Deuteronomistic[6] editor or author of the narrative in

[1] C. P. W. Gramberg (op. cit.) seems to have been the first to advance this theory.

[2] That a book was actually discovered was generally accepted by these scholars but there was no agreement as to its contents. Gramberg himself (op. cit. pp. 306f.) maintained that it was the Book of the Covenant in Exod. xx. 22–xxiii. 33; S. A. Fries believed that it was Exod. xxxiv (J); L. Seinecke (op. cit., vol. I, p. 387) argued that it was a short collection of Jeremiah's oracles. More recently (see below for their works) R. H. Kennett suggested that it may have been Exod. xxxiv or a collection of prophetic sayings. F. Horst argued that it was a prophetic book whilst G. Hölscher was not prepared to commit himself.

[3] R. H. Kennett, 'The Origin of the Aaronite Priesthood', *JTS* 6 (1905), pp. 161–186; idem, 'The Date of Deuteronomy', *JTS* 7 (1906), pp. 481–500; idem, *Deuteronomy and the Decalogue* (Cambridge, 1920), reprinted in *The Church of Israel* (ed. S. A. Cook, Cambridge, 1933), pp. 73–98; G. Hölscher, 'Komposition und Ursprung des Deuteronomiums', *ZAW* 40 (1922), pp. 161–255; idem, *Geschichte der jüdischen und israelitischen Religion* (Giessen, 1922), pp. 130–134; idem, 'Das Buch der Könige: seine Quellen und seine Redaktion', in *Gunkel Eucharisterion* in *FRLANT* 18 (1923), pp. 206–213; F. Horst, 'Die Anfänge des Propheten Jeremias', *ZAW* 41 (1943), pp. 94–153; idem, 'Die Kultusreform des Königs Josia', *ZDMG* 77 (1923), pp. 220–238; S. A. Cook, *C.A.H.*, vol. III (1925), pp. 406f. and 481–486; A. Loisy, *Religion d'Israel* (3rd edit., Paris, 1933), pp. 200ff.; Johs. Pedersen, *Israel: Its Life and Culture III–IV* (1940), pp. 569–592; W. Spiegelberg, 'Zur Datierung des Deuteronomiums', *OLZ* 26 (1923), pp. 481–482; F. C. Burkitt, in a review of Kennett's work, *JTS* 22 (1921), pp. 61–65; G. R. Berry, 'The Code found in the Temple', *JBL* 39 (1920), pp. 44–51; idem, 'The Date of Deuteronomy', *JBL* 59 (1940), pp. 133–139; J. N. Schofield, 'The Significance of the Prophets for the Dating of Deuteronomy', in *Studies in History and Religion* (ed. A. E. Payne, 1942), pp. 44–60.

[4] Cf. for example, E. Nielsen, *Oral Tradition* (London, 1954), pp. 56, 79; S. Mowinckel, *The Psalms in Israel's Worship*, I (Oxford, 1962) p. 4 n. 20.

[5] For a thorough discussion of this view see especially: L. B. Paton, op. cit.; H. Gressmann, 'Josia und das Deuteronomium', *ZAW* 42 (1924), pp. 313–337; K. Budde, 'Das Deuteronomium und die Reform König Josias', *ZAW* 44 (1926), pp. 177–224.

[6] We employ the word Deuteronomist when referring to the author of the corpus Deuteronomy-2 Kings and Deuteronomic when referring to the author of Deuteronomy itself.

Kings has altered or schematized the original account of the events of Josiah's reign. It is freely acknowledged by the advocates of this theory that the narrative in 2 Kings xxii–xxiii as it stands clearly intends Josiah's law book to be understood as having been Deuteronomy. But this, they argue, is due to the work of the Deuteronomist who intended to create this impression.[1]

G. Hölscher maintained that underlying the present narrative in 2 Kings xxii–xxiii is an original E narrative which he identified with the E document of the Pentateuch.[2] According to Hölscher this original E account has been worked over by redactors the last of whom was a Deuteronomist (Rd 2) who worked after 500 B.C. and by whom the narrative has been edited so as to make it appear that Josiah's book was Deuteronomy which had been composed, according to Hölscher, only a few years before this editor worked.[3] The crux of the matter is contained, he argues, in 2 Kings xxiii. 8a, 9 which narrates the destruction of the high places and the bringing up of the rural priests to Jerusalem. These two verses, he contends, interrupt an otherwise continuous account of the purification of the Temple in Jerusalem contained in verses 6–11; they deal not with Jerusalem and its immediate vicinity but go far beyond it. They were therefore no part of the original narrative and are without historical value. This being so, Hölscher concludes, the real reason for equating Josiah's book with Deuteronomy falls away. The original account of the events of Josiah's reign knew nothing of the removal of the high places in all Judah by Josiah; the real reformation was limited to Jerusalem.

R. H. Kennett took the view that the author of the narrative of Josiah's reign in 2 Kings xxii–xxiii was too far removed in time from the events described to be a reliable witness. He wrote after the fall of Judah in 586 B.C. and 'possibly considerably later'.[4] In view of this it is argued that 'there is no difficulty in supposing that the account of Josiah's reign, although based on a sound tradition, has

[1] Cf. for example, G. Hölscher, *ZAW* 40 (1922) p. 231; F. Horst, *ZDMG* 77 (1923), p. 221; R. H. Kennett, *Deuteronomy and the Decalogue* (1920), pp. 2f.; E. Nielsen, op. cit., p. 79: 'However, it was presumably no random guess that caused Deuteronomy to be identified with Josiah's law book. On the contrary, this was just what the author(s) of the Deuteronomic historical compilation wished every reader to do.'

[2] Hölscher believed that the sources used in the compilation of Kings were J and E up to the disruption of the monarchy (1 Kings xii. 19) and thereafter, up to the fall of Jerusalem, exclusively E. Cf. his 'Das Buch der Könige', *FRLANT* 18 (1923), pp. 206–213.

[3] Hölscher dated the composition of Deuteronomy about 500 B.C., about half a century later than E, which he believed also to be exilic.

[4] R. H. Kennett, *Deuteronomy and the Decalogue* (1920), p. 3.

been coloured by the belief that Josiah as a pious king must have acted in accordance with the Deuteronomic law'.[1]

Two major objections have been levelled against these arguments. The currently accepted view of the composition of the book of Kings is that it belongs to a Deuteronomistic history from Moses to the exile which begins in Deuteronomy and incorporates Joshua, Judges, Samuel and Kings.[2] Now the last event recorded in this history is the release of Jehoiachin from prison in exile by Amel Marduk in about 561 B.C. (2 Kings xxv. 27–30). There is no mention at all in Kings of any release of the Jews from exile, no hint of a return to Jerusalem or of the rebuilding of the Temple. If, as Hölscher maintains, the book of Kings was given its final shape by a Deuteronomistic editor after 500 B.C. then surely we would have had information on these events of such supreme importance for the Jews. This consideration has led the majority of commentators to fix the *terminus ad quem* for the composition of Kings and, *a fortiori*, for the Deuteronomistic history at 561 B.C. Some scholars have gone further and suggested that this short record of the release of Jehoiachin is an appendix added after the rest of Kings had been completed for some time.[3] On either view the narrative was written comparatively soon after the events described and it is, as H. H. Rowley has pointed out,[4] difficult to believe that the Deuteronomist would have issued what many would have realized immediately to be pure fiction concerning events which were still possibly within living memory.

An even more radical objection has been raised against the suggestion that the Deuteronomist portrayed Josiah as having promulgated Deuteronomy because he was, according to tradition, a pious king.[5] According to the standpoint of the Deuteronomist, Deuteronomy had been known to Israel since Moses. The kings of Israel and Judah are judged according to their loyalty to its demands, especially the abolition of the high places and the centralization of worship to Jerusalem. Of the kings before Josiah, Hezekiah alone is praised unconditionally for having obeyed its demands (2 Kings xviii. 5f.). Now it has been pointed out that consistency with this standpoint would have required that the Deuteronomist should record

[1] R. H. Kennett, op. cit., p. 3.
[2] Cf. M. Noth, *Überlieferungsgeschichtliche Studien I*[2] (Tübingen, 1957).
[3] Cf. for example, R. H. Pfeiffer, *Introduction to the Old Testament* (New York, 1948), p. 410; H. H. Rowley, 'The Prophet Jeremiah and the Book of Deuteronomy', *From Moses to Qumran* (1963), pp. 191f.
[4] H. H. Rowley, 'The Prophet Jeremiah and the Book of Deuteronomy', p. 192.
[5] Cf. G. Hölscher, 'Das Buch der Könige: seine Quellen und seine Redaktion', pp. 210f.; R. H. Kennett, *Deuteronomy and the Decalogue*, p. 3.

merely that Josiah, like Hezekiah, had acted in accordance with 'all the law of Moses' (cf. 2 Kings xxiii. 25).[1] What possible motive could he have had for describing Deuteronomy as having been actually discovered in Josiah's reign if in fact it had not been discovered?

These and other considerations have led the majority of commentators to reject the views of Hölscher, Kennett and other advocates of the theory of the exilic or post-exilic date for the composition of Deuteronomy and to accord historicity to the events recorded in 2 Kings xxii-xxiii whilst at the same time and on other grounds, as we shall see, holding reservations on the correct chronology of the events described. Today the view that Josiah's law book was the book of Deuteronomy in its original form is accepted by the majority of scholars.[2]

In one most important aspect, however, recent study has modified the theory as originally defined by De Wette and his successors. It is now being asked whether the reformation carried out by Josiah received its sole stimulus from the finding of the law book, as suggested by the narrative in 2 Kings, or whether part of it at least was implemented before the discovery of the law book and thus independently of it, as suggested by the narrative in 2 Chronicles xxxiv–xxxv which places significant reform measures before the year in which the book was found. Older scholars generally ignored the Chronicler's record as being of no historical value except in so far as it follows the narrative in Kings. More recently, however, this attitude has been considerably modified and it is now being increasingly accepted that the Chronicler may often preserve records from otherwise lost sources.[3] Recent discussion of Josiah's reform activities has paid more attention to the record in Chronicles and this has led to a completely new assessment of the relationship between the reformation and the law book.

[1] Cf. L. B. Paton, op. cit., p. 337.

[2] Attempts to equate Josiah's law book with the Holiness Code (G. R. Berry, 'The Code Found in the Temple', *JBL* 39, 1920, pp. 44–51. Cf. A. Freed's reply to this in 'The Code spoken of in 2 Kings xxii-xxiii', *JBL* 40, 1921, pp. 76–80), or with Deuteronomy plus the Holiness Code (Th. Oestreicher, *Das Deuteronomische Grundgesetz*, Gütersloh, 1923, pp. 22–24), or with the entire Pentateuch (cf. F. Dornseiff, 'Antikes zum Alten Testament: 4. Die Abfassungszeit des Pentateuch und die Deuteronomiumsfrage', *ZAW* 56, 1938, pp. 64–85; C. H. Gordon, *Before the Bible*, London, 1962, pp. 292f.) have been considered as unsuccessful by the majority of scholars.

[3] Cf. E. Sellin, *Einleitung in das Alte Testament*[8] (Heidelberg, 1950), p. 177; H. H. Rowley, 'Hezekiah's Reform and Rebellion', *Men of God* (London, 1963), pp. 98–132; A. S. Herbert, *Peake's Commentary*[2] (1962), p. 357; W. F. Albright, op. cit., p. 208; J. Bright, *A History of Israel* (London, 1960), p. 210 n. 3. In this work Bright frequently draws upon material peculiar to Chronicles.

We may begin our consideration of this new assessment by outlining briefly the differences between the account of Josiah's reign as contained in Kings and that in Chronicles. According to the former, Josiah in his eighteenth year on the throne carried out a reformation based on the demands of a law book which Hilkiah had found in the Temple in that same year (621 B.C.). The narrative implies that the reformation was due solely to this newly discovered book and began only after it had been found. The motive behind the reformation was the king's desire to implement the demands of this book; no movements towards reform were carried out prior to Josiah's eighteenth year as king.

Contrary to this sequence of events, the account in Chronicles records that Josiah had been carrying out reform measures in his twelfth year on the throne, that is, six years before the discovery of the book of the law. In this year the king, according to the Chronicler, 'began to purge Judah and Jerusalem from the high places, and the asherim, and the graven and molten images' (2 Chron. xxxiv. 3). We are further told that he carried this purge 'to the cities of Manasseh, Ephraim and Simeon as far as Naphtali' (xxxiv. 6). The account in Chronicles goes on to corroborate the narrative in Kings telling of the discovery of the law book in the eighteenth year of Josiah's reign, the king's dismay when he read it, and the subsequent consultation of the prophetess Huldah (xxxiv. 8ff.). But in the matter of the ensuing reformation recorded in Kings the Chronicler differs. Whereas Kings records Josiah as having carried out an extensive reformation which abolished the high places in Judah and northern Israel and of having rooted out pagan cults and practices, Chronicles, having dated these enactments in the twelfth year of Josiah's reign, narrates that only the making of a covenant (xxxiv. 29–32) and the celebration of the Passover (xxxv. 1–19) followed the discovery of the book; there is no mention of reforms after the finding of the book but only the purely general statement that the king 'took away all the abominations from all the territory that belonged to the people of Israel' (xxxiv. 33).

These two accounts are obviously at variance with one another. In the first place the chronology of events is different in the two narratives. In the second place, the law book is of much more significance in the Kings narrative than in Chronicles. Indeed, if only the account in Chronicles were extant then the evidence for equating Josiah's law book with Deuteronomy would be very slight. The problem raised therefore is that of determining exactly what the law book did contribute to the reformation.

The currently accepted view of the relationship between Deuteronomy and Josiah's reformation has its roots in the work of Theodor Oestreicher during the 1920s.[1] Oestreicher contended that the real motive behind the reformation was Josiah's desire to gain independence from the century-old Assyrian suzerainty.[2] He suggests that the first opportunity for doing so was occasioned by the death of Asshur-ban-apal which he dates in 627 B.C.—Josiah's twelfth year on the throne.[3] The Chronicler in recording the king as having carried out reforms in this year (2 Chron. xxxiv. 3–7) is therefore, according to Oestreicher, more accurate than the author of the narrative in Kings. Oestreicher proposes that in 627 B.C. Josiah purged Jerusalem of the Assyrian cult and that six years later in 621 B.C. further disturbances in Nineveh gave him the opportunity to continue its abolition throughout Judah.[4] During this year the law book was discovered and this, he continues, supplied further incentive to the king to complete the reformation. Thus, according to this hypothesis, Josiah's reformation was carried out in two distinct phases separated by six years and was motivated by politics; the law book was found long after the reformation had been inaugurated and was of only incidental significance;[5] and the narrative in 2 Kings xxii-xxiii has been schematized so as to make it appear that the real impulse for the reformation derived from the law book.

Whilst much of Oestreicher's thesis, particularly his narrow estimation of the significance of the law book in the reformation, has not carried conviction, it has in its broad outlines been accepted and supported by a considerable number of scholars in recent years.[6]

[1] Th. Oestreicher, *Das Deuteronomische Grundgesetz* (Gütersloh, 1923).

[2] Ibid., p. 39. Oestreicher qualified this, however, by stating that Josiah remained loyal to Assyria in external affairs. The evidence for this, he argued, is that Josiah met his death in attempting to intercept the advance of Necho's troops on Assyria in 609 B.C. (cf. 2 Kings xxiii. 29). We now know, however, that in fact Necho was marching to support Assyria against the Babylonians and that Josiah was killed whilst attempting to prevent the Egyptian forces from reaching Assyria. For this see D. J. Wiseman's extracts from 'The Babylonian Chronicle', *Documents from Old Testament Times* (ed. D. Winton Thomas, London, 1958), pp. 75f.

[3] Op. cit., p. 64.

[4] Ibid., p. 69.

[5] Ibid., p. 40; 'Die Auffindung des Thorahbuches . . . hatte in Wirklichkeit gar nicht die entscheidende Bedeutung die ihr heute zugeschrieben wird.'

[6] See for example: H. H. Rowley, 'The Prophet Jeremiah and the Book of Deuteronomy', *From Moses to Qumran*, p. 196; F. M. Cross and D. N. Freedman, 'Josiah's revolt against Assyria', *JNES* 12 (1953), pp. 56–58; W. A. L. Elmslie, *IB, III* (1954), pp. 537f.; G. E. Wright, *Biblical Archaeology*[2] (London, 1962), pp. 176f.; M. Noth, 'Die Gesetze im Pentateuch', now in his *Gesammelte Studien* (Munich, 1960), pp. 59f.; J. Bright, *A History of Israel*, p. 296; B. W. Anderson, *The Living World of the Old Testament* (London, 1958), p. 305; R. de Vaux, *Ancient Israel* (London, 1961), p. 337; G. von Rad, *Old Testament Theology*, I (London, 1962), pp. 75f.

The most notable statement of this theory has come from F. M. Cross and D. N. Freedman.[1] Their argument is briefly as follows.

The years after the death of Asshur-ban-apal witnessed the increasing weakening of the Assyrian empire until its collapse in about 612 B.C. Cross and Freedman base their suggestions on W. H. Dubberstein's chronology of the kings of Assyria during the seventh century.[2] Dubberstein fixed the date of Asshur-ban-apal's death at 633 B.C. and not later than 631 B.C. and arrived at the following chronology:

Asshur-ban-apal	669–633 B.C.
Asshur-etel-ilani	633–629 B.C.
Sin-shim-lisir	629 B.C.
Sin-shar-ishkun	629–612 B.C.

On the basis of this chronology Cross and Freedman argue that the account of Josiah's reform movements as related in 2 Chronicles xxxiv is supported by external evidence. Thus the annexation of the Assyrian provinces in northern Israel (2 Chron. xxxiv. 6) may have been occasioned by the death of Asshur-etel-ilani in 629 B.C. and the subsequent disorders in Assyria and Babylonia.[3] It is further suggested that the note in 2 Chronicles xxxiv. 3 which states that in the eighth year of his reign (632 B.C.) Josiah 'began to seek after the God of David his father' may indicate that he repudiated the gods of the Assyrian suzerain immediately following the death of Asshur-ban-apal in 633 B.C.[4] Finally, the events following the discovery of the law book in 621 B.C. are said 'to coincide precisely with the end of the last vestige of Assyrian control in Babylonia.'[5] It is therefore concluded that the dates supplied by the Chronicler (632, 628, 622 B.C.) correlate exactly with the major shifts in the fortunes of the Assyrian empire during the last years of its history.[6]

The main feature of the argument presented by Cross and Freedman, viz. that conditions lent themselves to revolt by Josiah before 621 B.C. and that the Chronicler's record of reformation before that year is historically trustworthy, is very plausible. It may be questioned, however, if it is wise to attempt to correlate the dates supplied

[1] Op. cit.

[2] W. H. Dubberstein, 'Assyrian-Babylonian Chronology', *JNES* 3 (1944), pp. 38–42.

[3] Cross and Freedman, op. cit., p. 57.

[4] Ibid., p. 57.

[5] Ibid., p. 56. It is suggested (ibid., p. 57 n. 1) that Josiah may have made common cause with the Babylonian rebels on the analogy of what Hezekiah had done one hundred years before in allying himself with Merodach-Baladan.

[6] Ibid., p. 58.

by the Chronicler with the major shifts in the fortunes of the Assyrian empire at that time. Such a correlation demands an accuracy in our dating of the Assyrian monarchs which we do not possess. For example, it is by no means certain, as Dubberstein suggested, that Asshur-ban-apal died in 633 B.C. Recently, dates of 629 B.C. and 627/6 B.C. have been advanced.[1] Where such uncertainty exists it is wiser to avoid basing conclusions upon precise but hazardous dates and to limit ourselves to more general and trustworthy statements concerning the events in the years before 621 B.C. In so doing we are on very safe ground. We can be sure that the last years of Asshur-ban-apal's reign and the years following his death were very troubled for the Assyrians,[2] and this would have been conducive to revolt in the subject countries. This itself favours the suggestion that Josiah began his reformation well before his eighteenth year on the throne (621 B.C.), as the Chronicler testifies, and that this reformation was an aspect of his assertion of sovereignty against the decaying Assyrian hegemony.

Some scholars have suggested that the narrative in 2 Kings itself may contain an indirect hint of pre-law book reforms. H. H. Rowley, for example, has pointed out that the fact that repairs were being carried out in the Temple before the law book was discovered may be an indication that the Jerusalem authorities had already been removing Assyrian cult emblems from it.[3] One further consideration substantiates the view presented here. It is very probable that Amon's assassination (2 Kings xxi. 19–26) was the work of an extreme anti-Assyrian party in Jerusalem, for according to both Kings and Chronicles Amon was as pro-Assyrian as his father Manasseh had been.[4] It is reasonable to infer, therefore, that there was a revolutionary party in the country which awaited a favourable opportunity to throw off the Assyrian yoke. Such an opportunity presented itself, as we have seen, in the years immediately before and after the death of Asshur-ban-apal and we can be sure that such a revolutionary party would not have let it pass by unexploited.

It may be concluded therefore that the Chronicler in so far as he

[1] A date of 629 B.C. is tentatively offered by A. L. Oppenheim in *IDB* I (New York, 1962), p. 257. H. W. F. Saggs suggests 627/6 B.C. in *The Greatness that was Babylon* (London, 1962).

[2] Cf. H. W. F. Saggs, op. cit., pp. 134ff.; A. L. Oppenheim, op. cit., p. 274.

[3] H. H. Rowley, 'The Prophet Jeremiah and the Book of Deuteronomy', op. cit., p. 196.

[4] Cf. A. Malamat, 'The Historical Background to the Assassination of Amon, King of Judah', *IEJ* 3 (1953), pp. 26–29. This position is followed by J. Bright, op. cit., pp. 294–295. Cf. B. W. Anderson, op. cit., p. 298; J. Mauchline, *Peake's Commentary*[2] (1962) p. 355.

records reform activity before the finding of the law book is historically trustworthy. To say this is not, however, to accord historicity to his chronological details of Josiah's reformation measures. It is clear, for example, that his schema has reduced to a minimum the role of the law book in the reformation since the really significant reforms are said to have been implemented before its discovery. In this the Chronicler has moved furthest from the standpoint of the author of the narrative in Kings for whom the law book was all important. Somehow a balance must be struck between the two accounts. In other words, which reforms preceded the discovery of the book and which followed it and were dependent upon its demands?

If the results of our investigation so far are accepted then it may be suggested that the reformation measures carried through by Josiah before 621 B.C. would have been motivated largely by the desire to gain independence from Assyria. They would thus have been concerned with getting rid of the Assyrian cult emblems and practices from the Temple in Jerusalem, where they would have been placed as a sign of Assyrian suzerainty, and the Judaean countryside (cf. 2 Kings xxiii. 4–5). At the same time it is also possible that other *foreign* cults were destroyed during this wave of resurgent nationalism. This would have consisted of the abolition of the Sidonian and Moabite cults noted in 2 Kings xxiii. 13.[1]

Part of Josiah's political ambitions seems to have been the conquest of northern Israel long since deprived of its monarchy and organized into provinces by Assyria. It is probable in fact that he revived the policy of Hezekiah to re-establish the boundaries of the all-Israelite state of the Davidic-Solomonic kingdom.[2] As to when he moved to take possession of the northern provinces we cannot be sure. It is possible that the opportunity for doing so came before 621 B.C.[3] But much of Josiah's time before this year must have been spent in consolidating the position of his own kingdom and if he did essay to expand northwards it can only have been shortly before 621 B.C. Very probably, however, it was after this year when his

[1] A. Jepsen, 'Die Reform des Josia', *Festschrift für Baumgärtel* (ed. J. Herrmann, Erlangen, 1959), p. 106 agrees that the removal of the Assyrian cult would have been motivated largely by political desires but suggests that the preaching of Zephaniah may have been a contributory factor in this and perhaps the main impulse behind the destruction of other cults including the Canaanite cults at this time.

[2] G. von Rad, *Old Testament Theology*, I (1962), p. 76 suggests that Josiah had the 'master picture of David's empire' before his eyes.

[3] So, for example, J. Bright, op. cit., p. 295; F. M. Cross and D. N. Freedman, op. cit., p. 57; B. W. Anderson op. cit., p. 305.

position in Judah was secure and the Assyrian empire already crumbling.[1]

The second stage of the reformation followed the discovery of and was based upon the demands of the law book. The central aim of this phase of the reformation was concerned with the purification of the Yahweh cult.[2] Josiah now abolished the high places throughout Judah and brought their priests up to Jerusalem (2 Kings xxiii. 8a, 9). All sorts of idolatrous cults and cultic practices were dealt with (2 Kings xxiii. 7, 8b, 10). It was also, as we have suggested, after 621 B.C. that he advanced northwards and extended the reformation to this territory (2 Kings xxiii. 15). This second phase of the reformation would have begun with a ceremony of the renewal of the covenant on the basis of the newly discovered 'book of the law' (2 Kings xxiii. 1–3).

On the basis of our conclusions the following schema of the events of Josiah's reign may be drawn up:

639 B.C. Josiah's first year on the throne.	
c. 630–621 B.C. The removal of the Assyrian and other foreign cults from Jerusalem and Judah. This first stage of the reformation was the outcome of the movement towards independence and national self-assertion.	2 Kings xxiii. 4–5, 11–13.
621 B.C. onwards: the discovery of the law book in the Temple and the implementation of the second phase of the reformation based upon the demands of this book. The extension of the boundaries of the Judaean kingdom to include the territory of the erstwhile northern state.[3]	2 Kings xxii; xxiii. 1–3, 8a, 9, 10, 15.
609 B.C. Josiah killed at Megiddo.	2 Kings xxiii. 29–30.

If these conclusions are accepted then it is clear that the Deuteronomistic author of the narrative in Kings has telescoped the reformation measures of Josiah's reign and has concentrated them in

[1] On this period see H. W. F. Saggs, op. cit., pp. 134ff., 140f.

[2] Cf. G. von Rad, *Old Testament Theology*, I (1962), pp. 75f. and 'Deuteronomy', *IDB*, I, (1962), p. 838.

[3] A. Jepsen, op. cit., p. 108 and M. Noth, *The History of Israel*[2] (London, 1960), pp. 273–274, both follow A. Alt, 'Judas Gaue unter Josia', *Kleine Schriften*, II (1953), pp. 276–288 and date the drawing up of the boundary lists of Judah (Joshua xv.) at this time. For a different view see F. M. Cross and G. E. Wright, 'The Boundary Lists of the Kingdom of Judah', *JBL* 75 (1956), pp. 202–226 where a ninth-century date for this is advanced. So too now R. de Vaux, op. cit., pp. 136–137.

the period following the discovery of the law book in 621 B.C., no doubt in order to press further the significance of the law book in the reformation. In view of this we must probably see in the account of the actual reformation (2 Kings xxiii. 4–14) a conflation of two originally separate short lists, perhaps derived from the court annals of Judah, of the reform measures of the two phases of the reformation. This would explain the apparent disorder in the narrative to which attention has often been drawn.[1]

One objection to the theory that Josiah carried out some reform measures before the discovery of the law book is that it involves a serious anachronism. W. Rudolph has argued that such a theory makes nonsense of Huldah's oracle (2 Kings xxii. 15–20) in which the nation is condemned for its idolatry and apostasy.[2] How could such a threat have been uttered if a reformation had only recently been carried out? Furthermore, if Josiah had been responsible for reforms before 621 B.C. then why did the prophetess not stipulate this action as that which would guarantee him safety from the impending doom instead of promising him deliverance because he had humbled himself when he read the book of the law (2 Kings xxii. 18f.)?

Such an objection, however, seems to presuppose that the oracle as it now stands represents the original words of the prophetess. The majority of commentators are agreed, however, that this is not the case and that the original oracle has been worked over by the Deuteronomistic historian of Kings. The oracle is composed of two addresses.[3] The first (2 Kings xxii. 15–17) is addressed to 'the man who sent you' and condemns the nation because of its apostasy and idolatry. The second (*vv.* 18–20) is addressed to 'the king of Judah' and whilst endorsing what the first address has already stated concerning imminent disaster, promises the king that he shall be buried in peace and shall not see the destruction of his kingdom and people. Of these two addresses the first contains some Deuteronomistic words and phrases and has been considered a *vaticinium post eventum*.[4] It seems to reflect the destruction of Judah recorded in chapter

[1] Cf. for example, A. Jepsen, op. cit., p. 98. This would also explain the awkward position of verses 8a and 9 upon which Hölscher based so much (see above p. 5). On the other hand, H. Schmidt in a review of Hölscher's work (*TLZ* 48, 1923, col. 290) argued that there has been an accidental displacement here. He suggested that a copyist accidentally wrote 8a immediately after 7 on account of the similar beginning of 7 and 8b; 8a therefore possibly stood originally after 8b immediately before verse 9 with which it is obviously connected.

[2] W. Rudolph, *Chronikbücher* (*HAT* ed. O. Eissfeldt, Tübingen, 1955), p. 319.

[3] The account of the oracle in Chronicles is substantially the same as that in Kings.

[4] Cf. for example, R. H. Pfeiffer, op. cit., p. 402.

xxiii. 26f. and as such may be a Deuteronomistic adaptation of Huldah's original oracle designed to fit in with the Deuteronomist's prophecy-fulfilment schema to which attention has been drawn.[1] Some have considered the second address (*vv.* 18–20) as authentic since it does not seem to be aware of Josiah's tragic death at Megiddo and promises him that he shall die 'in peace'.[2] As against this it may be argued that the word *šālōm* ('peace') here may refer not to the nature of Josiah's death but rather to the fact that he was to die whilst the *šālōm* or 'well-being' of his kingdom was still intact.[3] It also may therefore be a Deuteronomistic creation based upon the original oracle and intended to reflect what the ideal king's reaction to the law of Yahweh was.[4] What the original oracle was cannot therefore be precisely defined.[5] Most probably, however, it endorsed the demands of the law book and uttered some threat in keeping with the curses contained in the book. But there is no real inconsistency in all this. If the theory outlined in this chapter is accepted then the reform measures carried out before the discovery of the law book were largely of a political nature and did not satisfy the more radical and drastic requirements of the law book. The prophetess acknowledged this and uttered her oracle in the light of it.

Several important conclusions emerge from our discussion in this chapter. In the first place it has been affirmed that the attempt by such scholars as Hölscher, Kennett and Horst to dissociate Deutero-

[1] Cf. G. von Rad, *Studies in Deuteronomy*, pp. 78f.; idem, *Old Testament Theology*, I (1962), pp. 339f. Cf. J. Gray, *I & II Kings* (London, 1964), pp. 17f.

[2] Cf. J. A. Montgomery and H. S. Gehman, *Kings* (*ICC*, Edinburgh, 1951), p. 526.

[3] Cf. J. Gray, op. cit., p. 661.

[4] Cf. E. Nielsen, *Shechem: A Traditio-Historical Investigation*[2] (Copenhagen, 1959), p. 179.

[5] Several attempts have been made to isolate or reconstruct Huldah's original words from the oracle in its present form. Thus H. Gressmann ('Josia und das Deuteronomium', *ZAW* 42, 1924, p. 319) sought to determine the original oracle by rearranging and adding to the second address (*vv.* 18–20), the first address (*vv.* 15–17) being considered by him as secondary. He maintained that an editor has excised something which he found anachronistic in the original oracle. It is suggested that the opening words of the oracle may have been originally: 'Thus saith the Lord, the God of Israel: "The words which thou hast heard (concerning this place and its inhabitants, that they should become a desolation and a curse), *do I revoke. . . .*"' F. Horst ('Die Kultusreform des Königs Josia', *ZDMG* 77, 1923, p. 231) argued that the narrative of Josiah's reign has been compiled from two sources, A and B, of which A as the original and B a later unhistorical Deuteronomistic addition. He therefore sought to find the original oracle not in either of the two addresses but scattered throughout both of them. But such attempts to establish the *ipsissima verba* of the prophetess are bound to be highly subjective and few commentators today would accept them. For a critique of Gressmann's reconstruction of the oracle see my article 'II Kings xxii. 18—a simple restoration', *Hermathena* 97 (1963), pp. 96f.

nomy from Josiah's reformation cannot be considered successful. Thus the theory of De Wette in this respect at least has been substantiated. The vast majority of modern scholars accept this identification of Josiah's law book with Deuteronomy in its original form.[1] And this is of great significance in two ways. Firstly, it clearly establishes the *terminus ad quem* for the composition of Deuteronomy in 621 B.C. Secondly, it associates the promulgation of the book with the Jerusalem authorities. In this respect it is of importance in the discussion of the origin of the book. Did it originate in Jerusalem itself? Or if it had its origins elsewhere, then how did it come to be in Jerusalem in Josiah's reign? Whatever the answers to these problems may be, it is clear that the fact of the appearance of the book in Jerusalem and of its acceptance there on the part of the Judaean authorities must be accounted for in the discussion of its provenance and authorship.

At the same time recent research has modified De Wette's theory of the relationship between Josiah's reformation and Deuteronomy in at least one important respect. It is now generally accepted, as we have seen, that not all of the king's enactments are to be explained as deriving from the demands of the law book. It is probable that certain reforms, largely of a political nature, were carried out prior to the discovery of the book. Thus Deuteronomy must be seen as having played only a partial role, albeit an important role, in the total reformation movement of Josiah's reign. This too is of significance in the discussion of Deuteronomy. It rules out the possibility of the book having been designed as the 'blue print', so to speak, for that reformation. By the same token it is untenable to see it as the work of the Judaean reform and revival party of the seventh century since the aims of this group were already being implemented before the book made its appearance, unless of course it is argued that its 'discovery' in the Temple in 621 B.C. was a 'pious fraud' on the part of Hilkiah and the Jerusalem priesthood who wished to foist their own reformation programme upon the nation.[2] But quite apart from the fact that Deuteronomy is almost certainly not the work of the

[1] Thus H. H. Rowley, 'The Early Prophecies of Jeremiah' (first published in *BJRL* 45, (1963), pp. 198–234), now in his *Men of God* (London, 1963), pp. 133–168, can assert (p. 161): 'That Josiah's Law Book was Deuteronomy in some form, though not wholly identified with the present Book of Deuteronomy, seems to be one of the most firmly established results of Old Testament scholarship'. Cf. O. Eissfeldt, *The Old Testament: An Introduction* (Oxford, 1965), p. 173.

[2] J. Wellhausen seems to have held this view. Cf. his *Prolegomena to the History of Israel* (E. T. by J. Sutherland Black and A. Menzies, Edinburgh, 1885), pp. 25f.

Jerusalem priesthood,[1] such a view has not carried conviction among scholars and few today, if any, would subscribe to it.[2]

Here then we are left in possession of two vital factors in the discussion of the origin of Deuteronomy. The book must be seen as having been composed before 621 B.C. and as having been accepted and promulgated by the Judaean authorities in the reign of Josiah. How much of the present book of Deuteronomy lay before Josiah? How long before its discovery in 621 B.C. was it composed? In what circles and where did it originate? It is with these questions that we shall be concerned in the following pages.

[1] See below pp. 58ff., 93ff.

[2] Cf. for example, J. E. Carpenter and G. Harford, *The Composition of the Hexateuch* (London, 1902), p. 174; S. R. Driver, *An Introduction to the Literature of the Old Testament*[9] (Edinburgh, 1913), p. 87; G. A. Smith, *Deuteronomy* (*CBSC*, Cambridge, 1918), pp. xcix–c; H. H. Rowley, 'The Prophet Jeremiah and the Book of Deuteronomy', *From Moses to Qumran*, pp. 195–196; G. E. Wright, *Deuteronomy*, *IB* II (1953), p. 323; M. Noth, *The History of Israel*[2] (1960), p. 276 note.

CHAPTER II

THE STRUCTURE AND UNITY OF DEUTERONOMY

IT has been generally agreed that the book of Deuteronomy in its present form is the final outcome of a long literary growth beginning with the so-called *Urdeuteronomium* and developing through successive stages of literary expansion until it assumed its present dimensions. This view is based upon the presence in Deuteronomy of separate and apparently quite independent introductions and conclusions as well as other doublets and repetitions. But if general agreement has been reached on this, there has been at the other extreme the widest diversity of opinion on what parts of the present book constituted the original book and what parts are later additions.

In this chapter some attempt will be made to give a survey of the debate on this problem and to arrive at some tentative conclusions on the literary growth of the book. We may begin by outlining the structure and general contents of the book.

Deuteronomy takes the form of a series of sermons delivered by Moses to the Israelites on the eve of their entrance into the promised land. The book falls naturally into the following divisions:

(A) Chapters i-iv. 43: the first discourse prefaced by a short introduction (i. 1–5) and containing a historical retrospect (i. 6–iii. 29) and a hortatory section (iv. 1–40). This is followed by a short passage (iv. 41–43) which narrates in the third person the legislation concerning asylum cities on the other side of Jordan.
(B) The second discourse follows in chapters v–xi with a short introduction in iv. 44–49. This second address includes the decalogue (v. 1–21) and the *Shema*ʿ (vi. 4–5) as summaries of the law, with further hortatory material and a short historical section (ix. 7b-x. 11).
(C) These two introductory discourses are followed by the central legal section of the book (xii–xxvi.) which contains a selection of laws of very varied age and origin interspersed for the most part with parenetic material.
(D) The legal section finds its epilogue in chapter xxviii which proclaims blessings and curses which will befall Israel according to her faithfulness or unfaithfulness to the covenant stipulations just

laid down. Chapter xxvii, narrated in the third person, interrupts the connection between xxvi. 19 and xxviii and is widely regarded as secondary. It is closely related to Joshua viii. 30–35 and may therefore have been inserted into the book by the Deuteronomistic historian.[1]

(E) Chapters xxix–xxx contain yet another address of Moses insisting afresh upon faithfulness to the covenant demands.

(F) The final section (chs. xxxi–xxxiv.) contains a number of appendices to the book as follows:

(i) Moses's last words of encouragement (xxxi. 1–8).

(ii) The delivery of the law book to the levites with instructions for a ceremony of covenant renewal every seven years (xxxi. 9–13).

(iii) The commissioning of Joshua as Moses's successor (xxxi. 14–15, 23).

(iv) The Song of Moses (xxxii. 1–44) with an introduction in xxxi. 16–22, 24–30.

(v) The final commendation of the book to Israel (xxxii. 45–47).

(vi) The conclusion of the book containing the Blessing of Moses (xxxiii) and the narrative of his death (xxxiv).

Broadly speaking, two quite different solutions have been advanced by scholars in attempting to isolate the original book from the present book:

1. Many commentators, particularly in the earlier stages of the discussion, viewed the problem as one of deciding which of the main sections outlined above belonged to *Urdeuteronomium*. The debate centred largely on the problem of the plurality of introductory and concluding speeches: which of them, together with the central legal section in chapters xii–xxvi, constituted the original book?

2. Whilst many see the problem as being the same today, a greater number favour an attempt at the literary analysis of Deuteronomy along quite different lines. They seek to find the original book not in a combination of one of the introductory and concluding speeches with the law code in xii-xxvi, but in a combination of certain chapters and passages within several of the main sections of the book.

I

One of the most controversial problems in the debate concerning the unity of Deuteronomy has been the question of the two introductions to the book in chapters i–iv and v–xi. Both seem to be quite independent of one another. In the earlier stages of the discussion a

[1] See below p. 34.

number of scholars detected differences in style and standpoint between these two discourses and argued that the first section (i–iv) was a later addition to the original book to which the second discourse (v–xi) was the introduction proper.[1] On the other hand, an equal number of commentators contended that the differences stylistically and otherwise between the two sections are insignificant and not sufficient to warrant belief in different authorship.[2] Yet another body of opinion advocated the theory that the two introductory discourses were originally separate introductions to two separate editions of the law code in xii–xxvi.[3] Recently, however, fresh research into this problem has yielded a more satisfactory solution. In his monumental work on Deuteronomy and the Former Prophets,[4] Martin Noth has argued very convincingly that the first discourse, chapters i–iii (iv)[5] in Deuteronomy is not an introduction to that book but rather to the Deuteronomistic history of Israel from Moses to the exile contained in the corpus Deuteronomy–2 Kings.[6] Noth's suggestion is certainly the most attractive solution so far offered to this problem and has been widely accepted by scholars.[7] For the rest, it is agreed that chapters v–xi form either wholly[8] or in part[9] the original introduction to the book.

[1] Cf. for example, W. E. Addis, *The Documents of the Hexateuch*, I (London, 1892), p. lxv; J. E. Carpenter and G. Harford, *The Composition of the Hexateuch* (London, 1902), in a long footnote on pp. 155–158. See further G. A. Smith, *Deuteronomy* (*CBSC*, Cambridge, 1918), p. lix n. 2.

[2] So notably S. R. Driver, *Deuteronomy*[3] (1902), p. lxxii and *Introduction to the Literature of the Old Testament*[9] (1913), p. 94: 'The inconsistencies (between the two discourses), though they no doubt exist, are scarcely sufficiently serious to outweigh the strong impression produced by the predominant linguistic character of i–iv. 40, that it is by the same hand as ch. v ff.' See further G. A. Smith, op. cit., p. lxi n. 1.

[3] Notably J. Wellhausen, *Die Composition des Hexateuchs* (Berlin, 1899), p. 192 footnote: 'Chs. i–iv and v–xi have among other ends this one in common, to indicate a historical situation for the Deuteronomic legislation. They are properly two different prefaces to different editions (of the latter).' Wellhausen believed that *Urdeuteronomium* contained only the law code in chs. xii–xxvi. Cf. also O. Eissfeldt, *The Old Testament: An Introduction* (Oxford, 1965), pp. 231–232.

[4] M. Noth, *Überlieferungsgeschichtliche Studien I*[2] (1957). See below pp. 25f.

[5] M. Noth (ibid., pp. 14, 38f.) regards iv. 1–40 as a later expansion of an original Deuteronomistic nucleus.

[6] M. Noth, ibid., p. 14.

[7] Cf. for example: G. A. Danell, *Studies in the Name Israel in the Old Testament* (Uppsala, 1946), p. 51; G. E. Wright, *Deuteronomy, IB*, II (1953), p. 316; A. Bentzen, *Introduction to the Old Testament*[4] (Copenhagen, 1958), vol. II, pp. 23, 40; B. W. Anderson, *The Living World of the Old Testament* (1958), p. 310; G. W. Anderson, *A Critical Introduction to the Old Testament* (London, 1959), pp. 44, 53; J. A. Bewer, *The Literature of the Old Testament*[3] (revised edit. by E. G. Kraeling, New York and London, 1962), pp. 128, 229f.

[8] The entire section is accepted as original by G. E. Wright, *Deuteronomy, IB*, II, p. 317; B. W. Anderson, op. cit., pp. 310–311; G. W. Anderson, op. cit., p. 44; H. H. Rowley, *The Growth of the Old Testament* (London, 1950), p. 30.

[9] Noth himself regards certain parts of this section as secondary. See further below pp. 25f.

Virtually all scholars have agreed that the central legal section in chapters xii-xxvi formed the bulk of *Urdeuteronomium*.[1] Some suggested that it alone constituted the original book.[2] Others have argued that it also contains secondary material which has been added to an original nucleus.[3] It is widely accepted that the legal code finds its epilogue in chapter xxviii, chapter xxvii being usually regarded as a later insertion into the original book. Chapter xxviii. 1 seems to be closely connected with xxvi. 19 though it is possible that the original link between these two chapters was xxvii. 9–10.[4] Parts of chapter xxviii, however, seem to reflect the catastrophe of 586 B.C. and many commentators believe that it too has been subjected to a certain amount of expansion.[5]

Chapters xxix–xxx are of the nature of a supplement to the legal section and have generally been regarded as later additions to the original book.[6] Older critics viewed these two chapters as composite, though there was a willingness on the part of some to allot one or two short passages in them to *Urdeuteronomium*.[7] It has recently been suggested that these chapters on account of their marked liturgical form and interest—the recitation of the saving acts of God (xxix. 1–7), the solemn charge to accept the terms of the covenant (8–14), the stern warning of the consequences of apostasy and breach of the covenant (15–28), the promise of God's favour and mercy upon the nation if it truly repents and returns to him from such apostasy (xxx. 1–10), and finally the solemn appeal to the people to choose the way of life by entering into covenant with Yahweh (xxx. 11–14,

[1] J. Cullen, *The Book of the Covenant in Moab* (Glasgow, 1903), in contrast to the vast majority of scholars finds *Urdeuteronomium* not in the legal section but in the hortatory discourses. He takes the law code to be the deposit of Josiah's reformation. For a treatment of this view see G. A. Smith, op. cit., pp. xcvi-xcviii.

[2] Wellhausen and others believed the original book to have contained only the law code. For a bibliography see G. A. Smith, op. cit., p. xlvii footnote.

[3] F. Horst, 'Das Privilegrecht Jahwes', *FRLANT* 45 (NF 28), 1930, now in his *Gesammelte Studien* (Munich, 1961) pp. 17–154, analysed Deuteronomy xii–xviii and concluded that underlying it is an original pre-Deuteronomic document consisting of a decalogue representing Yahweh's 'Charter' (*Privilegrecht*) which has been subjected to a threefold expansion which in its final stage introduced the law of the centralization of the cult.

[4] Cf. S. R. Driver, *Deuteronomy*³ (1902), pp. 297–298; W. E. Addis, op. cit., p. lxxv; A. Bertholet, *Deuteronomium* (Leipzig, 1899), p. 84; recently G. Henton Davies, *Peake's Commentary*² (1962), p. 281.

[5] See below pp. 34f.

[6] There has been considerable debate as to whether xxviii 69 (EVV xxix. 1) is a subscription to xii–xxvi, xxviii or a superscription to xxix-xxx. Recently, however, the latter view has been widely preferred. Cf. G. E. Wright, *Deuteronomy*, *IB*, II (1953), p. 502; G. Henton Davies, op. cit., in loc.

[7] S. R. Driver, *Deuteronomy*³, p. lxxvi accepted xxx. 11–20 as original. G. A. Smith, op. cit., p. 329 and A. Bertholet, op. cit., p. 91 accepted xxx. 15–20. Cf. also E. Sellin, *Einleitung in das A.T.*⁸ (Heidelberg, 1950), p. 62.

15–20)—may be based upon an actual covenant ceremony (cf. xxxi. 9–13) which perhaps employed *Urdeuteronomium* as containing the covenant stipulations.[1] On the other hand there are some differences between xxix and xxx which suggest that they are not, as this view would suggest, a unity and for this reason may each belong to different stages in the growth of the book. We shall return to this at a later stage in our discussion.

That the final section, chapters xxxi–xxxiv, was not part of the original book but contains rather a series of appendices to it has been very widely accepted. They are considered as belonging less to the book of Deuteronomy proper than to the Pentateuch as a whole. The opinion of some earlier scholars that parts of these chapters form the link between the Pentateuch and Joshua[2] has been advocated more recently by Noth who sees in chapters xxxi. 1–13, 24–26a, and xxxiv, as in chapters i–iii (iv), the work of the Deuteronomistic historian.[3]

It may be concluded therefore that *Urdeuteronomium* contained at most chapters v–xxvi and much of xxviii of the present book. The problem now is one of deciding whether these chapters themselves contain any secondary material.

2

The question of the unity of chapters v–xxvi, xxviii leads us conveniently to a discussion of the second solution offered by some scholars in the attempt to isolate *Urdeuteronomium*. The main criterion employed by these scholars is the frequent transition from the singular to the plural form of address in Deuteronomy. It is believed that the changes in the form of address are accompanied by other changes in the narrative and on the basis of all this it is argued that the two forms of address, the second person singular and the second person plural, have different origins and different authors.

It was not until the last decade of the nineteenth century that this distinction in the form of address was carefully scrutinized. In 1891 C. H. Cornill regarded some laws as secondary on account of their use of the plural instead of the usual singular.[4] A few years

[1] Cf. G. E. Wright, *Deuteronomy*, *IB*, II (1953), pp. 317, 502; G. Henton Davies, op. cit., pp. 281–282.

[2] Cf. for example, G. A. Smith, op. cit., p. 332.

[3] M. Noth, *Überlieferungsgeschichtliche Studien I*[2] (1957), pp. 39–40.

[4] C. H. Cornill, *Einleitung in das A.T.* (Tübingen, 1891). Translated by G. H. Box from the 5th edition, *Introduction to the Canonical Books of the Old Testament* (London, 1907).

later, in 1894, W. Staerk[1] and K. Steuernagel[2] working independently published detailed analyses of Deuteronomy based upon the changing forms of address. Since then this criterion has been adopted by a large number of scholars and is currently favoured by many.[3]

Within the ranks of those who advocate the use of this linguistic criterion there have been two theories concerning the growth of Deuteronomy. The first, which was more characteristic at an earlier stage in the debate, sees in the present book of Deuteronomy the result of a combination of two or more originally separate editions (*Sonderausgaben*) of the original book, the one edition being in the singular and the other in the plural.[4] The second explains the development of Deuteronomy by way of a supplementary hypothesis whereby the original book was amplified by additions and expansions (*Ergänzungen* hypothesis) until it reached its present form.[5]

Of these two theories the first would find few supporters today since the problem of the plurality of introductory and concluding addresses from which this theory took its starting point is more satisfactorily accommodated by Noth's theory to which reference has already been made. More popular at present is the second theory, the supplementary hypothesis. This has been the subject of a most interesting recent study by G. Minette de Tillesse whose work we shall examine below. Before doing so, however, mention may first of all be made of some general objections which have been raised against the use of this linguistic criterion in the discussion of the literary analysis of Deuteronomy.

Right from the beginning it has met with vigorous opposition from a considerable number of scholars.[6] Broadly speaking, two main

[1] W. Staerk, *Das Deuteronomium: sein Inhalt und seine literarische Form* (1894).

[2] K. Steuernagel, *Der Rahmen des Deuteronomiums* (1894), and *Die Entstehung des deuteronomischen Gesetz* (1896).

[3] Cf. for example: H. Mitchell, 'The Use of the Second Person in Deuteronomy', *JBL* 18 (1899), pp. 61–109; J. Hempel, *Die Schichten des Deuteronomiums* (Leipzig, 1914); G. A. Smith, op. cit., pp. lxxiii ff.; G. Hölscher, 'Komposition und Ursprung des Deuteronomiums', *ZAW* 40 (1922), pp. 161–255; M. Noth, *Überlieferungsgeschichtliche Studien I*[2] (1957), pp. 16f.; J. H. Hospers, *De numeruswisseling in het Boek Deuteronomium* (1947); G. von Rad, *Studies in Deuteronomy* (1953), p. 11 n. 1; G. Minette de Tillesse, 'Sections "tu" et sections "vous" dans le Deutéronome', *VT* 12 (1962), pp. 29–87.

[4] So for example W. Staerk and J. Hempel in the works cited above. Cf. also O. Eissfeldt, op. cit., p. 232. K. Steuernagel attempted to find three originally separate editions of *Urdeuteronomium* now combined in Deuteronomy. For a critique of this see O. Eissfeldt, op. cit., pp. 225ff.

[5] Cf. especially G. Hölscher, 'Komposition und Ursprung des Deuteronomiums', *ZAW* 40 (1922), pp. 161–255; M. Noth, *Überlieferungsgeschichtliche Studien I*[2] (1957), pp. 16f.; J. H. Hospers, op. cit.; G. Minette de Tillesse, op. cit.

[6] Cf. W. E. Addis, *The Documents of the Hexateuch*, II (London, 1898), pp. 10f.; A. Bertholet, op. cit., p. xxi; J. E. Carpenter and G. Harford, op. cit., pp. 165f.;

objections have been levelled against it: (1) It has been argued that the divergencies between the readings in the MT and the other versions, particularly the LXX and the Samaritan text, render the criterion hazardous.[1] (2) Some commentators pointed to similar changes in the form of address in other parts of the Old Testament where there can be no question of plurality of authorship. Others further pointed to a similar usage in other semitic languages.[2]

Against the first objection it was contended that the differences between the LXX and the MT readings may be due to a 'harmonizing' process carried out by the LXX translators who deliberately sought to eliminate any sudden changes in the form of address in a given passage.[3] The evidence, however, does not point to this for there are many instances where the LXX follows the MT where one would expect harmonizing if such a process was carried out.[4] One can indeed go further and cite instances where the LXX has preserved a passage with both singular and plural in it as against a MT reading which is consistently either singular or plural.[5] Against the second objection, viz. that such changes in form of address are found in other parts of the Old Testament, it has been argued that there are reasons other than purely linguistic usage for these changes.[6] This same argument has been advanced in the case of Deuteronomy itself. That is to say, the linguistic criterion is not the sole basis of this method since, it is contended, other significant changes accompany the transition from the singular to the plural form of address.[7]

[1] Thus for example, in ch. i. 21 the MT has the singular in an otherwise plural passage whilst the LXX has the plural throughout. In ch. iv. 3 the MT is plural except for the last two words but the LXX and Peshitta have the plural throughout. Similarly in iv. 10 LXX is in the plural whilst MT is mixed (cf. also iv. 29). In vi. 3 the MT and LXX have one plural word as against the other versions which are singular throughout. Cf. also the differences between the MT and LXX in chs. vi. 17, viii. 1, x 15, xi. 13, 14, etc.

[2] Cf. especially A. Sperber, op. cit.

[3] So for example A. F. Puukko, *Das Deuteronomium* (Leipzig, 1910), pp. 105f.; J. Hempel, op. cit., pp. 7–15; G. A. Smith, op. cit., pp. lxxv f.

[4] Cf. for example in both MT and LXX chs. i. 31, ii. 24, vi. 3, vii. 4, 25, etc.

[5] Cf. for example in MT and LXX vi. 18, ix. 1, xvi. 3, etc.

[6] Cf. G. A. Smith, op. cit., pp. lxxviif.

[7] G. Minette de Tillesse, 'Sections "tu" et sections "vous" dans le Deutéronome', *VT* 12 (1962), p. 34.

J. Cullen, op. cit., pp. 2–4; E. König, *Das Deuteronomium* (1917); J. Sperber, 'Der Personenwechsel in der Bibel', *Zeitschrift für Assyriologie* 32 (1918), pp. 23–33; S. Mowinckel, *Le Décalogue* (Paris, 1927), p. 14; B. D. Eerdmans, 'Deuteronomy' *Old Testament Essays* (ed. D. C. Simpson, London, 1927), pp. 78–84; H. M. Wiener, 'Zur Deuteronomiumsfrage', *Monatschrift für Geschichte und Wissenschaft des Judentums*, N.F. 36 (1928), pp. 28–48; H. Breit, *Die Predigt des Deuteronomiums* (Munich, 1933); A. Bentzen, *Introduction to the Old Testament*[4] (1958), II p. 41; G. E. Wright, *Deuteronomy*, *IB*, II (1953), pp. 362, 393f.; A. Weiser, *Introduction to the Old Testament* (1961), p. 130.

The most recent treatment of Deuteronomy from this point of view has come from G. Minette de Tillesse.[1] De Tillesse takes his starting point from Noth's theory that the corpus Deuteronomy–2 Kings represents the work of a Deuteronomistic author who wrote the history of Israel from Moses to the release of Jehoiachin in exile about 561 B.C. Noth believes that this massive work was written by one man who wished to present to his generation a theological interpretation of the catastrophes of 721 B.C. and 586 B.C. The entire work is designed to show that the downfall of Israel was the direct consequence of apostasy and the constant failure to obey the divine demands (cf. 2 Kings xvii. 7ff.).

The history is divided into five periods. The first is the Mosaic period and is covered by the book of Deuteronomy. Here the Deuteronomist has incorporated, according to Noth, the original book of Deuteronomy as containing the law of Yahweh as mediated through Moses. The main purpose of the history is to show that it was Israel's refusal down through the centuries to remain faithful to the covenant demands as set forth in 'the law of Moses' which led ultimately to her downfall. The second period, contained in the book of Joshua, narrates the period of the conquest under Joshua.[2] This is followed by the history of the Judges (Judges–1 Sam. vii) which ends with the rise of the monarchy. The history of the monarchy is subdivided into two periods. The first (1 Sam. viii–1 Kings viii) records the rise of the monarchy under Saul and its zenith under David and Solomon with the building of the Temple. The final period is the record of the increasing apostasy under the monarchy in both northern and southern kingdoms and the ultimate downfall of both states, the north in 721 B.C. and Judah in 586 B.C.

Noth, as we have observed, regards Deuteronomy i–iii (iv) as the prologue to this history and parts of the last four chapters of the book as the link between Deuteronomy and Joshua. For the rest, he believes that Deuteronomy iv. 44–xxx. 20 lay before the Deutero-

[1] Ibid.

[2] The major difficulty in Noth's thesis is his denial that except for D Joshua contains any of the Pentateuchal sources. It is well known that he regards the corpus Genesis–Numbers as a Tetrateuch (cf. his *Überlieferungsgeschichte des Pentateuch*, Stuttgart, 1948) and would limit its extent to these books and one or two short passages at the end of Deuteronomy. But most scholars are agreed, against Noth, that the Tetrateuch in both its J and E strands looks forward to the gift of the land (cf. Gen. xii (J) and xv (E)) as the fulfilment of the promise to the Patriarchs. Consequently it is widely agreed that underlying Joshua i-xi is an original JE narrative which completed the Tetrateuch narrative of God's election of Israel and his gift to her of the promised land. For a discussion see J. Bright, *Joshua*, *IB*, II (1953), pp. 541ff.

nomistic historian more or less as we now have it, although he holds that *Urdeuteronomium* consisted of the singular portions of this block which have been subsequently surcharged with the plural passages now present in it.[1] De Tillesse now goes further than Noth and attempts to demonstrate that in fact the plural passages within iv. 44–xxx. 20 are also the work of the Deuteronomist.

De Tillesse's work is divided into three sections. In the first[2] he attempts to show that most of the plural passages in Deuteronomy v–xxvi[3] (chs. v. 1–vi. 1; vi. 14, 16–17a; vii. 4, 5, 7–8a, 12a, 25a; viii. 1, 19b–20; ix. 7b–x. 11; x. 15c–19; xi. 2–32; xii. 1–12; xiii. 1a, 4b–5, 6b, 8a, 14b (EVV xii. 32a; xiii. 3b–4, 5b, 7a, 13b); xvii. 16–20) can be removed as simple glosses in an otherwise coherent singular text. In the second section[4] he draws attention to close literary parallels between these plural passages in Deuteronomy and the style of the Deuteronomistic historian as found throughout the books of Joshua, Judges, Samuel and Kings. Finally, he attempts to show that the theology of the plural passages is the same as that of the Deuteronomist.[5]

For the purposes of this discussion we have chosen to deal with the second and third sections, the literary and theological parallels, first. If de Tillesse is correct then this will establish a literary and theological connection between the plural passages in Deuteronomy and the work of the Deuteronomist. We shall then be in a position to discuss the relationship of the plural sections to the singular sections in Deuteronomy itself from a literary critical point of view (de Tillesse's section one).

The most perplexing difficulty in attempting to analyse the literary growth of Deuteronomy is the remarkable homogeneity in language, style and ideology which pervades the book. It is precisely this which has given rise to such diversity of opinion on the contents of *Urdeuteronomium* and the secondary additions to it.[6] Careful examination of the style of the book will reveal an impressive array of similarities between chapters i–iv, v–xxx and the Deuteronomistic sections in xxxi–xxxiv.[7] By contrast, the differences between the various divisions in the book are slight, amounting to no more than a nuance in

[1] M. Noth, *Überlieferungsgeschichtliche Studien I*[2], p. 16.
[2] G. Minette de Tillesse, op. cit. pp. 34–47.
[3] De Tillesse confines his discussion for the most part to chs. iv. 44–xxvi.
[4] Ibid., pp. 47–73.
[5] Ibid., pp. 73–86.
[6] Thus no less a scholar than S. R. Driver believed that i–iv were written by the same author as v–xxvi. Cf. his *Deuteronomy*[3] (1902), p. lxxii.
[7] For a list of similarities see G. A. Smith, op. cit., pp. liiiff.

syntax or at most a short phrase. In view of this it can only be concluded that almost the entire book derives from people who, however separated in time they may have been from each other, had this very striking style and mode of expression in common.

In spite of this difficulty, however, de Tillesse has presented a most attractive analysis of the singular and plural passages in Deuteronomy and by comparing them with Deuteronomistic texts in Joshua–2 Kings and the commonly accepted Deuteronomistic passages in Deuteronomy itself (i–iii, xxxi. 1–13, 24–26a, xxxiv) has made what must be considered a strong case for his basic thesis.[1]

Deuteronomy xii. 1–12 is composed in the plural[2] and has been regarded by a number of commentators as a later additon to the original book.[3] These verses open the legal section proper by demanding the destruction of all Canaanite high places and the centralization of the worship of Yahweh to one sanctuary and thus, by implication, the abolition of all other Yahweh shrines. The law concerning the centralization of the cult is formulated in the plural (xii. 5) and the singular (xii. 14) as follows:

xii. 5 כי אם־אל־המקום אשר־יבחר יהוה אלהיכם מכל־שבטיכם

xii. 14 כי אם־במקום אשר־יבחר יהוה באחד שבטיך

Of the two phrases מכל־שבטיכם and באחד שבטיך, the latter never occurs in any Deuteronomistic passage whilst the former is paralleled by מכל שבטי ישראל in 1 Kings viii. 16, xi 32, xiv. 21; 2 Kings xxi. 7.[4] Another striking parallel between this plural passage in Deuteronomy and the Deuteronomist is to be found in the familiar expression in xii. 2 ועל־הגבעות ותחת כל־עץ רענן. This expression

[1] It may be noted that Noth himself has approved of Minette de Tillesse's basic principle. Cf. de Tillesse, op. cit., p. 34 n. 3.

[2] Only a very few words are in the singular (*vv.* 1, 5, 7, 9). In *vv.* 5, 9 all the versions agree in reading the plural. The singular phrase in *v.* 7 may be an addition (cf. *Biblia Hebraica*, in loc.).

[3] Cf. for example, A. C. Welch, *The Code of Deuteronomy* (London, 1924), pp. 194f. where xii. 1–7 are regarded as secondary; G. A. Smith, op. cit., p. 159. Cf. G. von Rad, *Deuteronomium* (*ATD*, Göttingen, 1964), p. 66.

[4] De Tillesse, op. cit., pp. 66f. De Tillesse (ibid.) suggests that the expression מכל־שבטיכם is a deliberate attempt to reinforce באחד־שבטיך which he believes to be less definite and possibly tolerant of an interpretation which would legalize a plurality of altars. Such a view was advocated at an earlier time by A. C. Welch, *The Code of Deuteronomy*, pp. 48f. and 'The two descriptions of the sanctuary in Deuteronomy', *ExpT* 36 (1925), pp. 442–444 and *ExpT* 37 (1926), pp. 215–219, and by Th. Oestreicher, *Das Deuteronomische Grundgesetz*, pp. 103f. and 'Dtn. xii 13f. im Licht von Dtn. xxiii 16f.', *ZAW* 43 (1925), pp. 246–249. But such an interpretation of the phrase in xii. 14 is unwarranted. For a discussion of this point see below pp. 53f.

never occurs in a singular passage but is exactly paralleled in 2 Kings xvi. 4 and very closely in 1 Kings xiv. 23 and 2 Kings xvii. 10:

Deut. xii. 2	ועל־הגבעות ותחת כל־עץ רענן
2 Kings xvi. 4	ועל־הגבעות ותחת כל־עץ רענן
1 Kings xiv. 23	על כל־גבעה גבהה ותחת כל־צץ רענן
2 Kings xvii. 10	על כל־גבעה גבהה ותחת כל־עץ רענן

Both the polemic against the paraphernalia of the Canaanite cult and the demand for centralization are constant preoccupations of the Deuteronomist.[1] The centralization of worship in Jerusalem and the consequent abolition of the high places is nothing less than the obsession of the author of Kings who pronounces judgment upon each king according to his obedience or disobedience to this law. In view of this and the linguistic parallels referred to above it is reasonable to suppose that the Deuteronomist has inserted here at the beginning of the legal section in Deuteronomy his own formulation of the law so central to his theology.

The central aim of the Deuteronomistic historian is concerned with providing a theological interpretation of the collapse and downfall of Israel in 721 B.C. and 586 B.C. He achieves this by selecting from the traditions at his disposal and presenting them within a framework which demonstrates how Israel sank deeper and deeper into apostasy and disobedience until Yahweh finally rejected her. G. von Rad has shown that part of the author's technique is his use of a prophecy-fulfilment schema whereby events in a given period of Israel's history are seen to be the fulfilment of prophetic predictions of an earlier period.[2] Thus, for example, the downfall of the northern kingdom is recorded in 2 Kings xvii. 23 as the fulfilment of a prophetic prediction noted in verse 13 of the same chapter. Similarly, the destruction of Judah is seen to be the fulfilment of predictions made in Manasseh's reign (cf. 2 Kings xxi. 10f. with xxiv. 2f.). Closely associated with this genre of prophetic predictions are the various threats of exile which occur in passages here and there throughout the Deuteronomistic corpus: Deuteronomy iv. 26f., vi. 15, vii. 4, viii. 19–20, xi. 17, xxviii. 36f., 63f., xxix. 27f., xxx. 18–19; Joshua xxiii. 13, 16; 1 Kings ix. 6 f.; 2 Kings

[1] For the former see 2 Kings xviii. 4; xxiii. 4; etc. See further G. Minette de Tillesse, op. cit., p. 66 for parallels between Deut. xii. 3, vii. 5 (both plural) and 2 Kings xi. 18, xviii. 4, xxiii. 4.

[2] G. von Rad, *Studies in Deuteronomy*, pp. 78ff.

xvii. 13, xxi. 10f. Of these, Deuteronomy iv. 26f. together with the references in Joshua and Kings are from the Deuteronomist. Deuteronomy vi. 15 and vii. 4 are both in the singular form of address and certainly belong to *Urdeuteronomium*. On the other hand viii. 19b–20, xi. 17[1] are both in the plural and are, unlike vi. 15 and vii. 4, closely parallel in language and phraseology to Joshua xxiii. 13 and Deuteronomy iv. 26:[2]

Joshua xxiii. 13: עד־אבדכם מעל האדמה הטובה הזאת אשר נתן לכם יהוה אלהיכם

Joshua xxiii. 16: וחרה אף־יהוה בכם ואבדתם מהרה מעל הארץ הטובה אשר נתן לכם

Deut. iv. 26: העידתי בכם היום את־השמים ואת־הארץ כי־אבד תאבדון מהר מעל הארץ אשר אתם עברים את־הירדן שמה לרשתה

Deut. viii. 19: העדתי בכם היום כי אבד תאבדון

Deut. xi. 17: וחרה אף־יהוה בכם ...... ואבדתם מהרה מעל הארץ הטבה אשר יהוה נתן לכם

Deut. vi. 15: פן־יחרה אף־יהוה אלהיך בך והשמידך מעל פני האדמה

Deut. vii. 4: וחרה אף־יהוה בכם והשמידך מהר

The historical section ix. 7-x. 11 is, with the exception of only a few words,[3] written in the plural and has been regarded by a number of commentators as secondary.[4] It comprises four parts:

1. The incident of the golden calf ix. 7–22 (23–24);
2. Moses's prayer of intercession ix. 26–x. 5;
3. a short historical allusion to Israel's wandering x. 6–7;
4. the levites are commissioned to bear the Ark of the Covenant x. 8f.

The main purpose of the narrative is to demonstrate how Israel has been disobedient from the beginning:

> 'You have been rebellious against the Lord from the day that he[5] knew you.'
>
> (Deut. ix. 24)

[1] Cf. also Deut. xxx. 18–19 and see de Tillesse, op. cit., pp. 52f.

[2] Cf. de Tillesse, op. cit. pp. 52f. The plural sections almost always employ the verb אבד when speaking of Israel's possible destruction whilst the singular passages generally use the verb שמד. The plural passages use the latter verb when referring to nations other than Israel. Cf. de Tillesse, ibid., p. 55.

[3] In ix. 7. Cf. *Biblia Hebraica*.

[4] Cf. G. A. Smith, op. cit., in loc.; G. von Rad, *Deuteronomium* (*ATD*, 1964) in loc.

[5] Following the LXX against the MT 'since I knew you'.

From this standpoint it therefore accords well with the central aim of the Deuteronomistic historian to which reference has already been made. The section abounds with linguistic parallels with the Deuteronomist's style and phraseology. The following are a few of those listed by de Tillesse: Deuteronomy ix. 7 'until you came to this place you have been rebellious against the Lord'. The expression 'until you came to this place' occurs only here and in Deuteronomy i. 31, xi. 5. The verb מרה with the meaning of 'rebel against God' is used exclusively in the plural sections and by the Deuteronomist (cf. Deut. ix. 7, 23, 24; i. 26, 43; 1 Sam. xii. 14, 15; 1 Kings xiii. 21, 26). Deuteronomy ix. 12 'they have turned aside quickly (סרו מהר) out of the way which I commanded them'. The verb סור with the meaning of 'turn aside (from the commandments of Yahweh)' is employed only in the plural passages and by the Deuteronomist (cf. Deut. v. 32, xvii. 20; Joshua i. 7, xi. 15, xxiii. 6; 1 Kings xv. 5, xxii. 43; 2 Kings xviii. 6, xxii. 2). Deuteronomy ix. 25 'I lay prostrate before the Lord' occurs frequently in the Deuteronomist (cf. Joshua v. 14, vii. 6, 10; 1 Sam. v. 3f., xxv. 23, xxviii. 20; 2 Sam. ix. 6, etc.). In the expression 'I prayed to the Lord' (Deut. ix. 26) the verb פלל in the hithpa'el is used as it is in the Deuteronomist (cf. 1 Sam. i. 10, 12, 26, 27, ii. 1, 25, vii. 5, viii. 6, xii. 19, 23; 2 Sam. vii. 27; 1 Kings viii. 29, 30, 33, 35, 42, 44, 48, 54, xiii. 6; 2 Kings iv. 33, vi. 17, 18). These literary parallels between this plural passage in Deuteronomy and the work of the Deuteronomist substantiate further de Tillesse's thesis.[1]

The incident of the making of the golden calf was certainly of considerable significance for the Deuteronomist. The setting up of the golden calves at Bethel and Dan by Jeroboam I (1 Kings xii. 26f.) was, as far as he was concerned, the sin *par excellence* of the northern kingdom. Each king is roundly cursed for 'walking in the sins of Jeroboam the son of Nebat' and the downfall of the northern state is ultimately attributed to this (cf. 2 Kings xvii. 21f.). It has long been recognized that the narrative in Deuteronomy ix. 7 f. is dependent upon Exodus xxxii[2] and that in their present form both are aimed against the actions of Jeroboam I.[3] In the light of this de Tillesse now plausibly suggests that the Deuteronomist has inserted

[1] Cf. further de Tillesse, op. cit., pp. 56–63.

[2] For a list of parallels between the two narratives see S. R. Driver, *Deuteronomy*³ (1902), pp. 112f.

[3] Cf. A. R. S. Kennedy, 'Golden Calf', in *HDB* (Edinburgh, 1898), vol. I, p. 341; S. R. Driver, *Exodus* (*CBSC*, Cambridge, 1918), p. 346; D. M. G. Stalker, *Peake's Commentary*² (1962), p. 238; M. Noth, *Exodus* (London, 1962), p. 246.

the narrative of the golden calf into the Mosaic period to prefigure the apostasy of the northern kingdom.[1]

One other significant point emerges from the discussion of this section. Attention has recently been drawn to the small role played by the Ark in Deuteronomy.[2] What must be of considerable significance is the fact that it is never mentioned in the singular passages of the book but only here in this plural passage (x. 1–5) and in xxxi. 9, 25f. If, as we shall see, Deuteronomy derived from the northern kingdom then this is understandable since the Ark was removed permanently to Jerusalem by David some three to four centuries before Deuteronomy made its appearance.[3] If de Tillesse's thesis is correct then this treatment of the Ark in Deuteronomy x and xxxi must be viewed as the Deuteronomist's attempt to give the Ark, which had retained its importance in the specifically Jerusalem theology by which he was influenced, some place in his work.[4] But it is important to note that in so doing he has reduced it to a mere receptacle for the tables of the law and has robbed it of its significance as the throne of the invisibly present Yahweh which it seems to have had in the traditions specifically associated with Jerusalem.[5] This is undoubtedly due to the influence of the so-called 'name-theology' of Deuteronomy and the Deuteronomist which excludes any notion of Yahweh himself dwelling on earth.[6]

It is unnecessary to weary the reader with further examples of literary and theological parallels between the plural sections in Deuteronomy and the work of the Deuteronomistic historian. De Tillesse has dealt very thoroughly with the entire problem. It is hoped, however, that enough has been said to suggest at least the strong probability that the Deuteronomist who, on Noth's generally accepted theory, was responsible for Deuteronomy i–iii (iv), xxxi. 1–13, 24–26a, xxxiv, is also the author of most of the plural passages within chapters v–xxx.[7]

If this hypothesis is accepted then the problem of the literary growth of Deuteronomy is rendered considerably less difficult. It is now possible to see chapters i–iv, parts of xxxi–xxxiv as well as the

Conclusion ✓

[1] G. Minette de Tillesse, op. cit., p. 60.
[2] Cf. G. von Rad, *Studies in Deuteronomy*, p. 40.
[3] Cf. F. Dumermuth, 'Zur deuteronomischen Kulttheologie und ihre Voraussetzungen', *ZAW* 70 (1958), pp. 59–98, esp. pp. 70f.
[4] For the relationship of the Deuteronomist to the Jerusalem traditions see Chapter VI below.
[5] G. von Rad, *Studies in Deuteronomy*, p. 40 says aptly that Deuteronomy has 'demythologized' the Ark.
[6] Cf. G. von Rad, ibid., pp. 37ff. and below pp. 55f.
[7] On exceptions to this see de Tillesse, op. cit., pp. 40f.

majority of plural passages within chapters v–xxx as the work of the Deuteronomistic author of the great history work contained in the corpus Deuteronomy–2 Kings. For the rest, the singular passages in v–xxvi probably belonged for the most part to the original book which this Deuteronomistic historian has incorporated into his work. It is possible, however, that the legal section in chapters xii–xxvi has been expanded to some extent at least from an original nucleus. The strongest evidence for this is the fact that the material does not seem to follow any orderly arrangement. This is particularly true of chapters xxi–xxv which contain a miscellany of laws:

Ch. xxi. 1–9 the case of an unsolved murder;
10–14 the treatment of women prisoners of war;
15–17 the rights of inheritance;
18–21 the case of a rebellious son;
22–23 a law governing the body of a criminal who has been hanged.

Ch. xxii. 1–4 laws governing the return of lost property;
5 an old law forbidding women to wear men's clothing and *vice versa*.
6–7 a law concerning a bird's nest which has been found;
8 a command to build balustrades on house tops;
9–11 old cultic laws forbidding 'mixtures' of seed in a vineyard, animals for ploughing, or material for garments;
12 a law commanding fringes to be made on every garment;
13–xxiii. 1 (EVV xxii. 30) laws dealing with sexual purity;

Ch. xxiii. 2–9 (EVV 1–8) laws governing admission to the *Qahal;*
10–15 (EVV 9–14) old Holy War laws concerning cleanness in the camp;

Ch. xxiii. 16–xxv. 19 a series of widely differing laws.

Chapters xii–xvi. 17 and xvi. 18–xviii. 22 are less mixed. The first section deals largely with laws pertaining to correct worship as against idolatry whilst the second deals with laws concerning various officials. Here again, however, there are incongruities in content. Thus for example in xiv. 3–21 there is a series of food laws[1] and in xv. 1–18 laws concerning the release. In the section dealing with

[1] Ch. xiv. 3–20 may be a later insertion based upon Lev. xi. 2–23. Cf. G. A. Smith, op. cit., p. 183; G. Minette de Tillesse, op. cit., p. 40.

officials, xvi. 21–xvii. 7 introduces once more the subject of the cult and idolatry.

This lack of order in Deuteronomy xii–xxvi has so far defied solution. It is possible that some obvious repetitions are later additions (cf. xiii. 1–5 with xviii. 21–22). It has also been observed that from chapter xx onwards the amount of parenesis, so characteristic of Deuteronomy, decreases and it has been suggested that some parts of these chapters may on this account be later additions.[1] On the other hand, they contain several laws concerning war which have at their basis old norms pertaining to the Holy War. G. von Rad has demonstrated how largely the ideology of the Holy War figures in Deuteronomy as a whole[2] and in view of this these laws at least are probably original. But beyond these few remarks, little more can be said concerning chapters xii–xxvi.

It is questionable, however, if it is possible, as de Tillesse believes, to remove the plural passages within v–xxvi without damage to the narrative. Some of them can no doubt be excised (e.g. vi. 14, 16) but others can be extracted only at the expense of continuity in the narrative. Thus, for example, vii. 5 (plural) follows on from verse 4 and links up with verse 6:

> 'For he would turn away thy son from following me, to serve other gods; and the anger of the Lord would be kindled against you, and he would destroy thee quickly. But thus shall you deal with them: you shall break down their altars, and dash in pieces their pillars, and hew down their Asherim, and burn their graven images with fire. For thou art a people holy to the Lord thy God; the Lord thy God has chosen thee to be a people for his own possession, out of all the peoples that are on the face of the earth.'

Similarly, vii. 12b (singular) would be meaningless without 12a (plural):

> 'And because ye hearken to these ordinances, and keep and do them, the Lord thy God will keep with thee the covenant and the steadfast love which he swore to thy fathers.'

Again, it is impossible to remove without disrupting the narrative the plural passage in viii. 19–20:

> 'And if thou shalt forget the Lord thy God and go after other gods and serve them and worship them, I solemnly warn you this day that you shall surely perish. Like the nations that the Lord makes to perish

[1] Cf. G. von Rad, *Studies in Deuteronomy*, p. 22.

[2] G. von Rad, ibid., pp. 45–59. Cf. further his *Der Heilige Krieg im alten Israel* (Göttingen, 1958), pp. 68ff.

before you, so shall you perish, because you would not obey the voice of the Lord your God.'

The most reasonable position to adopt is that the Deuteronomist using *Urdeuteronomium* as his source has inserted short comments here and there and in other places actually reshaped slightly the text to incorporate his own thoughts, at times perhaps replacing the original (singular) text by his own (plural) rendering.[1]

We may, before concluding, take a further look at chapters xxvii–xxx. Chapter xxvii, as we have already noted, clearly breaks the connection between xxvi. 19 and xxviii. Its secondary nature is further evidenced by the fact that it is cast in the third person and not in the second person form of address characteristic of Deuteronomy as the direct speech of Moses. The chapter comprises three distinct sections. Verses 1–8 make provision for a ceremony to take place at Shechem between Mts. Ebal and Gerizim when the Jordan is crossed. This ceremony, involving the erection of stones upon which the law is to be inscribed as well as an altar for sacrificial worship, is recorded as having been carried out in Joshua viii. 30–35. Verses 9–10 form a short unit which has no connection with what precedes since it deals not with prescriptions for later occasions but with the present, announcing that 'this day' Israel has become the people of God. It bears all the marks of having originated within a cultic setting and may well form the continuation and conclusion of xxvi. 17–19.[2] Verses 11–26 form the final section in this chapter and provide for a liturgical ceremony involving the setting forth of blessings and curses when the Jordan has been crossed. The ceremonies legislated for in this chapter are, as we have noted, recorded as having been executed in Joshua viii. 30–35 and it is not unreasonable to suppose therefore that this chapter comes from the Deuteronomist who constructed it on the basis of older materials.[3]

Chapter xxviii has been taken by most commentators to have belonged to *Urdeuteronomium*.[4] Certainly it follows logically after xxvi or, if they are accepted as original, xxvii. 9–10. The chapter sets forth the blessings and curses which will befall Israel according to her faithfulness or unfaithfulness to the covenant demands. Of the chapter, verses 1–14 contain a list of blessings and verses 15–68

[1] The attempt to recover *Urdeuteronomium* down to verse and half verse must be abandoned.

[2] Cf. G. von Rad, *Deuteronomium* (*ATD*, Göttingen, 1964), pp. 118–119.

[3] For a discussion of this chapter see G. von Rad, ibid., pp. 117f.

[4] Cf. S. R. Driver, *Deuteronomy*[3] (1902), p. lxv; M. Noth, *Überlieferungsgeschichtliche Studien I*[2], p. 17.

the curses. The section containing the curses is thus almost four times as long as that dealing with the blessings. In view of this and the fact that it contains clear reflections of the bitter experiences of 586 B.C. (cf. *vv.* 36f., 49f., 64f.) many commentators suggest that the chapter has been considerably expanded by an exilic editor.[1]

Chapter xxx would seem to be the logical continuation of xxviii. It takes up again the singular form of address interrupted by xxix and proclaims that even after the curses outlined in xxviii have befallen Israel, God will have mercy upon her and will restore her from exile if she acknowledges her sins and returns to him. It is interesting to note that this chapter contains a short passage in the plural form of address (*vv.* 18, 19a) which is reminiscent of the plural passages in v–xxvi.[2] If these few phrases in the plural are, as de Tillesse suggests,[3] a Deuteronomistic insertion, then this chapter must have been part of the book which lay before the Deuteronomist. It is possible therefore that an exilic editor has expanded the original chapter xxviii and has added to it, in the same style, what is now chapter xxx.

Chapter xxix begins properly with xxviii. 69 (MT) and introduces a fresh address of Moses. It begins with a recollection of Yahweh's mighty acts in Egypt and his grace towards Israel during the wilderness wandering (*vv.* 1–7, EVV 2–8). It continues with a general exhortation to obedience to the covenant demands (*v.* 8, EVV 9) and some verses (*vv.* 9f., EVV 10f.) which seem to presuppose a covenant ceremony. The remainder of the chapter contains warnings of the disastrous consequences of apostasy. Verses 21f. (EVV 22f.) seem to reflect the calamities of 586 B.C. and its aftermath. Here again it is not unlikely that the Deuteronomist has inserted this chapter composed as it is for the most part in the plural form of address.

It will be clear from our discussion that the history of the literary growth of Deuteronomy is exceedingly complex and in the last analysis impossible to trace with any real certainty in all its stages. Recent research has rightly abandoned the old attempt to isolate the original nucleus of the book down to verse and half verse.[4] In the light of our survey, however, we may propose the following tentative suggestion as the development of the book.

[1] Cf. especially G. von Rad, *Deuteronomium*, pp. 124f.
[2] Cf. de Tillesse, op. cit., pp. 52f.
[3] Ibid., pp. 53–54.
[4] Cf. O. Eissfeldt, *The Old Testament: An Introduction* (1965), p. 176.

(A) The original book consisted for the most part of the singular passages within chapters v–xxvi together with some of chapter xxviii.
(B) Chapter xxviii was subsequently expanded after the fall of Jerusalem in 586 B.C. and chapter xxx added to it.
(C) The Deuteronomistic historian has then incorporated this book into his history and provided it with a framework in chapters i–iii (iv), xxxi. 1–13, 24–26a, xxxiv (Noth). At the same time he surcharged the original singular passages in v–xxvi with most of the plural passages now in these chapters (de Tillesse) and has probably also added chapters xxvii and xxix.
(D) This block of material was subjected to further editorial expansion at a later stage when part of chapter xxxi as well as chapters xxxii and xxxiii were added. These additions may have been made when Deuteronomy was united with Genesis–Numbers to form the Pentateuch.

This examination of the growth of Deuteronomy has revealed that the book assumed its present form only gradually and over a considerable period of time. In discussing the origin and authorship of Deuteronomy it is clearly necessary to distinguish as far as possible between the original book and the later additions to it since these additions may reflect a different standpoint from the authors of the original book and misguide us in our discussion of this problem.

CHAPTER III

THE NATURE OF DEUTERONOMY AND THE TRADITIONS UPON WHICH IT STANDS

THE problems surrounding the date, authorship and provenance of Deuteronomy are amongst the most controversial in the study of the Old Testament. At one time or another almost every period in Israel's history from Moses to the exile has been advocated as the date for its composition,[1] whilst its authorship has at various times been attributed to Moses, Samuel, levitical priests, the Jerusalem priesthood, or prophetic circles.[2] Similarly, the origin of the book has been traced to Jerusalem, Shechem, Bethel, and elsewhere.[3]

[1] The Mosaic authorship of Deuteronomy has been advocated recently by J. Reider, *Deuteronomy* (London, 1937); G. T. Manley, *The Book of the Law: Studies in the Date of Deuteronomy* (London, 1957); idem, *The New Bible Dictionary* (ed. J. D. Douglas, London, 1962), p. 308; E. J. Young, *An Introduction to the Old Testament* (revised edit., London, 1964), p. 94ff.; M. H. Segal, 'The Composition of the Pentateuch: a fresh examination', *Scripta Hierosolymitana*, vol. VIII (Jerusalem, 1961), pp. 68–114. E. Robertson proposed that the book was drawn up under the guidance of Samuel as the standard law book for the centralized administration brought about by the advent of the monarchy under Saul. Cf. his collected studies *The Old Testament Problem* (Manchester, 1950), p. 138. A similar view was advanced by R. Brinker, *The Influence of Sanctuaries in Early Israel* (Manchester, 1946). A. C. Welch advocated a tenth-century date in his *The Code of Deuteronomy: a new theory of its origin* (London, 1924), and *Deuteronomy: the framework to the Code* (London, 1932). Cf. also Th. Oestreicher, *Das Deuteronomische Grundgesetz* (Gütersloh, 1923). F. Dornseiff, 'Antikes zum Alten Testament: 4. Die Abfassungszeit des Pentateuch und die Deuteronomiumsfrage', *ZAW* 56 (1938), pp. 64–85 argued for a ninth-century date for the entire Pentateuch. F. Dumermuth, 'Zur deuteronomischen Kulttheologie und ihre Voraussetzungen', *ZAW* 70 (1958), pp. 59–98 suggested a date sometime before the fall of the northern kingdom in 721 B.C. Cf. also J. Bowman, 'The Samaritans and the Book of Deuteronomy', *TGUOS* 17 (1958), pp. 9–18. The seventh-century date is still favoured by the majority of scholars. An exilic or early post-exilic date has been favoured by Kennett, Hölscher, Pedersen, Berry, Cook, Schofield, Mowinckel, Nielsen, etc. (See above p. 4 notes 3, 4.)

[2] For the Mosaic authorship see the works of Reider, Manley, Young and Segal referred to in the previous footnote. For Samuel see E. Robertson, op. cit. and R. Brinker, op. cit. That Deuteronomy originated among circles of levites has been suggested by A. Bentzen, *Die josianische Reform und ihre Voraussetzungen* (Copenhagen, 1926); G. von Rad, *Studies in Deuteronomy* (1954); cf. also G. E. Wright, *Deuteronomy, IB* II (1953), pp. 325 ff.; H. W. Wolff, 'Hoseas geistige Heimat', *TLZ* 81 (1956), pp. 83–94 now in his *Gesammelte Studien* (Munich, 1964), pp. 232–250, esp. p. 248. F. Dornseiff, op. cit., argued that an individual levite composed the book. R. H. Pfeiffer, *Introduction to the Old Testament* (1948), pp. 179f. suggested that a member of the Jerusalem priesthood compiled Deuteronomy. S. R. Driver, *Deuteronomy*[3] (1902), favoured a prophetic origin as also did K. Budde, 'Das Deuteronomium und die Reform des Königs Josia', *ZAW* 44 (1926), pp. 177–224 and, more recently, A. Weiser, *Introduction to the Old Testament* (1961), p. 132.

[3] At an earlier stage in the discussion the book was associated with Jerusalem,

Of these problems, the first, the question of the date of the composition of Deuteronomy, has been the least contentious in recent years. The seventh-century date has prevailed among the vast majority of commentators. But the remaining two problems, the authorship and origin, are still very open questions. Recently a northern Israelite provenance of the book has been widely favoured[1] although a Judaean or more specific Jerusalem origin have both been argued.[2] At the same time, an increasing number of scholars have accepted the view that the book owes its origins to circles of levites.[3]

In what follows we shall be concerned with the more recent research into this twofold problem of the origin and authorship of Deuteronomy. In this chapter some attempt will be made to outline the nature of the book from the point of view of the traditions which underly it and to isolate its peculiar demands and characteristics. This is obviously a necessary prolegomenon to the study of the problem of where and amongst what circles it originated.

One of the most important results of the form-critical investigation

[1] Notably by the following: A. C. Welch, *The Code of Deuteronomy* (London, 1924); A. Alt, 'Die Heimat des Deuteronomiums', *Kleine Schriften*, II (1953), pp. 250–275; W. F. Albright, *From the Stone Age to Christianity*[2] (1946) p. 241; A. Weiser, *Introduction to the Old Testament* (1961), p. 132; G. E. Wright, *Deuteronomy* in *IB* II (1953), pp. 323–326; J. Bowman, op. cit.; F. Dumermuth, op. cit.; J. Bright, *A History of Israel* (1960) pp. 299–300; G. Henton Davies in *Peake's Commentary*[2] (1962), p. 269; H. Ringgren, *Israelitische Religion* (Stuttgart, 1963), p. 150. C. F. Burney, *The Book of Judges* (London, 1918), in a footnote on p. xlvi suggested that it originated among prophetic circles in northern Israel and expressed the intention of publishing an elaboration of this under the title *The Prophetic School of Northern Israel and the Mosaic Tradition.* As far as I am aware, however, this work never appeared.

[2] Cf. G. von Rad, *Studies in Deuteronomy* (1954), pp. 60–69; O. Bächli, op. cit.

[3] Cf. especially G. von Rad, *Studies in Deuteronomy;* G. E. Wright, *Deuteronomy* in *IB*, II (1953); H. W. Wolff, op. cit.; A Bentzen, *Die josianische Reform*, (1926); F. Dumermuth, op. cit.

---

mainly on account of the demand for the centralization of the cult. Recently the same view has been advanced by O. Bächli, *Israel und die Völker: eine Studie zum Deuteronomium* (Zürich, 1962). In recent years many have argued that the book originated in Shechem. Cf. W. F. Albright, *From the Stone Age to Christianity*[2] (Baltimore, 1946), p. 241; G. A. Danell, *Studies in the Name Israel in the Old Testament* (Uppsala, 1946), p. 56; I. Engnell, *Symbolae Biblicae Uppsalienses*, vii (1946), pp. 21f.; R. Brinker, op. cit., pp. 211f.; A. Alt, 'Die Heimat des Deuteronomiums', *Kleine Schriften*, II (Munich, 1953), p. 274 n. 1; B. W. Anderson, *The Living World of the Old Testament* (1958), p. 309; E. Nielsen, *Shechem: A Traditio-Historical Investigation*[2] (Copenhagen, 1959), pp. 45, 85. Others have favoured Bethel. Cf. W. O. E. Oesterley and T. H. Robinson, *Introduction to the Books of the Old Testament* (1934), p. 54; J. N. Schofield, '"All Israel" in the Deuteronomic Writers', *Essays and Studies Presented to S. A. Cook* (ed. D. Winton Thomas, London, 1950), p. 27; F. Dumermuth, op. cit., pp. 79f.; J. A. Bewer, *The Literature of the Old Testament*[3] (1962), p. 131. G. von Rad, *Studies in Deuteronomy* (1954), pp. 60f. traces the immediate origin of Deuteronomy to circles of levites in the Judaean countryside.

of the Old Testament carried out in recent years has been the increasing emphasis placed upon the influence of cultic worship upon the origin and form of much of its literature. This has led, for example, to a complete transformation in our understanding of the origin of the Psalms which are now seen to have been composed for the most part for communal worship and not, as previously believed, for private and individual use.[1] Similarly, a new appreciation of the relationship between the prophets and the cult has come about and it is now widely accepted that the great canonical prophets if not themselves cultic functionaries[2] derived much in both the form and content of their preaching from the cult.[3] And when we turn to the Pentateuch and the Former Prophets, here again the cultic origin or basis of much of their contents has been stressed.[4] There is to be sure a growing feeling that the liturgical element is being over emphasized and that more caution has to be exercised in this field of investigation.[5] Nevertheless, the basic principle is now firmly established and widely accepted.

With this new understanding of the importance of cultic worship in the formation of the literature of the Old Testament has come a wider definition of its scope. By cultic worship scholars now mean not only the performance of the sacrificial rites prescribed in the Pentateuch but also the larger festivals celebrated at various times during the year in ancient Israel. There is still a great deal of con-

[1] Cf. for example, S. Mowinckel, *Psalmenstudien I–VI* (1921–24), and his more recent *The Psalms in Israel's Worship* (Oxford, 1962), I, ch. 1; A. Weiser, *The Psalms* (London, 1962). For an introduction to recent study see H. Ringgren, *The Faith of the Psalmists* (London, 1963). For the older point of view see Oesterley and Robinson, op. cit., pp. 194f. where it is argued that less than half of the Psalms were used in public worship.

[2] Even this has been argued, notably by A. Haldar, *Associations of Cult Prophets among the Ancient Semites* (Uppsala, 1945). Haldar's views have, however, been regarded as too extreme by the majority of scholars mainly because he fails to emphasize the distinctive features of Israelite prophecy.

[3] For this see S. Mowinckel, *Psalmenstudien III: Kultprophetie und prophetische Psalmen* (rep. Amsterdam, 1961), and *The Psalms in Israel's Worship* (Oxford, 1962), II, pp. 53 ff.; A. R. Johnson, 'The Prophet in Israelite Worship', *ExpT* 47 (1935–36), pp. 312ff. and *The Cultic Prophet in Ancient Israel*[2] (Cardiff, 1962); J. Lindblom, *Prophecy in Ancient Israel* (Oxford, 1962), pp. 78f., 206f. *et passim*; H.-J. Kraus, *Worship in Israel* (Oxford, 1966), pp. 101ff.; R. E. Clements, *Prophecy and Covenant* (London, 1965), pp. 19f. *et passim*.

[4] Cf. especially, G. von Rad, 'Das formgeschichtliche Problem des Hexateuch,' *BWANT* IV: 26 (Stuttgart, 1938), now in his *Gesammelte Studien* (Munich, 1958), pp. 9–86; Johs. Pedersen, 'Passahfeste und Passahlegende', *ZAW* 52 (1934), pp. 161ff.; M. Noth, *Überlieferungsgeschichte des Pentateuchs* (Stuttgart, 1948); A. Weiser, *Introduction to the Old Testament* (1961); H.-J. Kraus, *Worship in Israel* (1966); W. Beyerlin, *Origins and History of the Oldest Sinaitic Traditions* (Oxford, 1965); M. Newman, *The People of the Covenant* (New York, 1962).

[5] For a critical assessment of this trend see G. E. Wright, 'Cult and History', *Interpretation* 16 (Jan. 1962), pp. 3–20.

troversy concerning the number and form of these festivals.[1] But it is being increasingly recognized that the most important, at least in the pre-exilic period, was the Feast of Tabernacles which was celebrated in the autumn. The nature and form of this festival, especially as it was celebrated in the Jerusalem Temple during the period of the monarchy, have been the subject of considerable controversy.[2] But there is a large amount of agreement that in the period of the tribal league it took the form of a festival of covenant renewal.[3] It is with this festival that Deuteronomy has, as we shall see, close ties and it is therefore necessary to examine it briefly here.

It is the German scholar G. von Rad who has been foremost in the attempt to reconstruct the form and content of this old amphictyonic festival.[4] Von Rad maintains that there were two major festivals in early Israel. The one centred on the Sinai traditions and was a festival of the renewal of the covenant, whilst the other consisted of a celebration of the exodus-conquest traditions.

Von Rad takes his starting point from the concise historical credal statements which now appear in later contexts in the Old Testament but which had their original *Sitz im Leben* in the cult of the amphictyonic period.[5] The theme of these little credos is a *Heilsgeschichte*—a summary of Yahweh's saving deeds on Israel's behalf in history. Deuteronomy xxvi. 5b–9 is such a creed:

Dt 26

'A wandering Aramaean was my father; and he went down into Egypt and sojourned there, few in number; and there he became a nation,

[1] Cf. G. E. Wright, ibid.

[2] Some scholars, particularly A. Weiser, *The Psalms* (London, 1962), pp. 26ff., argue that the festival in Jerusalem took the form of the older amphictyonic covenant renewal festival. S. Mowinckel, on the other hand, believes that it was essentially a festival of the Enthronement of Yahweh. Cf. his *Psalmenstudien II. das Thronbesteigungsfest Jahwes und der Ursprung der Eschatologie* (rep. Amsterdam, 1961). In his more recent work, *The Psalms in Israel's Worship*, I and II (Oxford, 1962), however, he has placed more emphasis on other aspects of the festival, such as covenant renewal. H.-J. Kraus, *Die Königsherrschaft Gottes im Alten Testament* (Tübingen, 1951), has argued that the festival in Jerusalem celebrated the bringing of the Ark there by David and the establishing of the Davidic monarchy. He rejects Mowinckel's thesis concerning the enthronement of Yahweh, arguing that this is a late development dependent upon the teaching of Deutero-Isaiah.

[3] Cf. G. von Rad, 'Das formgeschichtliche Problem des Hexateuch', *Gesammelte Studien* (1958), pp. 41ff. and *Old Testament Theology*, I (1962), pp. 17f.; A. Alt, 'Die Ursprünge des israelitischen Rechts', *Kleine Schriften*, I (1953), pp. 327ff.; J. Bright, *A History of Israel* (London, 1960), p. 149; A. Weiser, *Introduction to the Old Testament* (1961), pp. 89ff.; W. Eichrodt, *Theology of the Old Testament*, I (London, 1961), pp. 122f.; M. Newman, *The People of the Covenant* (New York, 1962), pp. 112f.; W. Beyerlin, *Origins and History of the Oldest Sinaitic Traditions* (Oxford, 1965), pp. 40f.

[4] G. von Rad, 'Das formgeschichtliche Problem des Hexateuch,' *Gesammelte Studien*, esp. pp. 28ff., 41ff.

[5] Cf. G. von Rad, ibid., pp. 11ff.

great, mighty, and populous. And the Egyptians treated us harshly and afflicted us and laid upon us hard bondage. Then we cried unto the Lord the God of our fathers and the Lord heard our voice, and saw our affliction, our toil, and our oppression; and the Lord brought us out of Egypt with a mighty hand and an outstretched arm, with great terror, and with signs and wonders; and he brought us into this place and gave us this land, a land flowing with milk and honey.'

A similar confession is to be found in Deuteronomy vi. 20–24:

'When your son asks you in time to come saying: What is the meaning of the testimonies and the statutes and the ordinances which the Lord our God has commanded you? then you shall say to your son: We were Pharaoh's slaves in Egypt; and the Lord brought us forth out of Egypt with a mighty hand; and the Lord showed signs and wonders, great and terrible, against the Egyptians and against Pharaoh and all his household, before our eyes; and he brought us out from there, that he might bring us in and give us the land which he swore to our fathers. And the Lord commanded us to do all these statutes, to fear the Lord our God, for our good always that he might preserve us alive, as at this day.'

We may add to these Joshua's speech before the assembly at Shechem (Joshua xxiv. 2b-13) which follows the same pattern.[1]

Although the details vary, a fixed scheme underlies all of these passages—God called Israel's fathers and promised them the land, delivered them from bondage in Egypt and, after their wandering in the wilderness, gave them the promised land. This credo theme appears elsewhere in the Old Testament in prayers, cult lyrics and narrative (e.g. 1 Sam. xii. 8; Ps. lxxviii; cv; cxxxv; cxxxvi). Now it is striking that never in these credal statements is there any mention of the Sinai covenant events. Von Rad concludes from this that the two themes, the exodus-conquest and the Sinai, had separate liturgical histories and were joined together only at a relatively late date.[2]

Originally the Sinai events were, according to von Rad, the subject of a separate festival. In the Sinai pericope in Exodus xix-xxiv he distinguishes four parts of an ancient covenant renewal ceremony:[3]

[1] Ibid., pp. 14f.

[2] Von Rad (ibid., pp. 60f.) argues that the Yahwist first joined the two traditions together. M. Noth (*Überlieferungsgeschichte des Pentateuch*, pp. 40ff) holds that they were already united in G which he believes underlies the work of both J and E. For a critique of Noth's position see J. Bright, *Early Israel in Recent History Writing* (London, 1956), pp. 79ff.

[3] G. von Rad, 'Das formgeschichtliche Problem des Hexateuch', *Gesammelte Studien*, pp. 35f.

1. Parenesis (xix. 4–6) and historical presentation of the Sinai events (xixf.).
2. The promulgation of the law (Decalogue and Book of the Covenant).
3. The promise of blessing (xxiii. 20f.).
4. The making of a covenant (xxiv).

According to von Rad this renewal of the covenant festival had its *Haftpunkt* at the old tree sanctuary of Shechem (cf. Deut. xxvii; Joshua viii. 30f.; xxiv) and was celebrated in the autumn at the Feast of Tabernacles,[1] whilst the exodus-conquest celebrations (the credo theme) were held at Gilgal in the Jordan valley and were the festival-legend of the Feast of Weeks.[2]

This radical separation by von Rad of the Sinai covenant traditions from the exodus-conquest election traditions has been vigorously challenged by a number of scholars and it has been questioned whether his assessment of the *Sitz im Leben* of the credo theme is correct.[3] Several important objections have been raised against it.

It has been pointed out that both themes are present in Joshua's speech to the assembly at Shechem (Joshua xxiv), the first part of the address comprising the credo theme (*vv.* 2–13) and the second part (*vv.* 14–25) the covenant traditions.[4] Von Rad would isolate the first part from the second but this can hardly be valid. Here surely the two sets of tradition are closely combined and supplement one another. The recitation of the *Heilsgeschichte* is given as the prolegomenon to the exhortation to serve Yahweh (*vv.* 14–15), the people's pledge to do so (*vv.* 16–18), and finally the actual covenant ceremony (*vv.* 25f.). In other words we have already here a renewal of the covenant ceremony in which the recitation of Yahweh's saving deeds in history played a vital role.

But furthermore, to separate the election theme from the covenant demands robs the latter of all motivation. It was precisely because of what Yahweh had done on Israel's behalf that she undertook to serve him.[5] By the same token the election theme itself would become

[1] G. von Rad, op. cit., pp. 41ff. [2] Ibid., pp. 48ff.

[3] Cf. especially A. Weiser, *Introduction to the Old Testament*, pp. 83ff.; W. Beyerlin, *Origins and History of the Oldest Sinaitic Traditions* (Oxford, 1965). Beyerlin's work is the most thoroughgoing critique of von Rad's thesis thus far offered.

[4] Cf. A. Weiser, *Introduction to the Old Testament*, pp. 87f.

[5] Cf. M. Newman, *The People of the Covenant* (1962), pp. 21f.; N. W. Porteous, 'Actualization and the Prophetic Criticism of the Cult', *Tradition und Situation: Studien zur alttestamentlichen Prophetie* (Festschrift für A. Weiser, ed. E. Würthwein and O. Kaiser, Göttingen, 1963), p. 95; R. E. Clements, *Prophecy and Covenant* (1965), pp. 54f.

devoid of any real meaning, for the covenant can only be seen as the natural outcome of Yahweh's choice of Israel at the exodus. It was the covenant at Sinai which defined the relationship between Israel and Yahweh, the elected-elector relationship, brought about by the deliverance from bondage.

These objections against von Rad's thesis have been strikingly substantiated by recent research into the form and content of ancient near eastern covenant formulations, particularly the suzerainty treaties of the Hittite empire of the late bronze age (1400–1200 B.C.). G. E. Mendenhall has established that there are remarkable similarities in form between these Hittite treaties and the covenantal formulations of the Old Testament.[1] He isolates six basic elements in these treaties.[2]

1. The treaty begins with the identification of the king who is offering the treaty: 'Thus (saith) NN, the great king, king of the Hatti land, son of NN . . . the valiant.' This is clearly paralleled in early covenant passages in the Old Testament in which God addresses the people: 'I am the Lord . . . ' (e.g. Exod. xx. 1–2. Cf. Joshua xxiv. 2).

2. There follows a historical retrospect which lays particular emphasis on the past deeds of kindness wrought by the suzerain on behalf of the vassal. This was no doubt aimed at invoking the vassal's grateful response to the ensuing treaty obligations. It is also clearly paralleled in the Old Testament where preceding the promulgation of the covenant law there is a historical sketch of what Yahweh has done for his people. It may be a brief summary such as we find in the preamble to the Decalogue in Exodus xx. 2 'I am the Lord your God, who brought you out of the land of Egypt, out of the house of bondage'. Or it may be a somewhat longer account of the *Heilsgeschichte* such as is given in Joshua xxiv. 2–13.

3. The first two sections are the prolegomena to the central section, the presentation of the laws laid down by the suzerain and consisting of the obligations imposed upon the vassal accepting the treaty. This is paralleled in the Old Testament by the Decalogue and the Book of the Covenant in Exodus xx. 22–xxiii. 33 and in Deuteronomy xii–xxvi. In this connection it is very significant that usually the basic feature of the treaties is the demand that the vassal shall acknowledge only the rule of the suzerain offering the treaty.[3] This

[1] G. E. Mendenhall, 'Covenant Forms in Israelite Tradition', *BA* XVII (September 1954), no. 3. For an excellent summary see G. E. Wright, *Biblical Archaeology*[2] (1962), pp. 100f. Cf. also W. Beyerlin, op. cit., pp. 50ff.

[2] The form is not rigid and occasionally one or other of the elements may be lacking. Cf. G. E. Mendenhall, op. cit., p. 58.

[3] Cf. G. E. Mendenhall, op. cit., p. 59; W. Beyerlin, op. cit., pp. 52f.

feature is strikingly paralleled in the Old Testament where the first law in the Decalogue is 'You shall have no other gods before me'.

4. The treaties provided for the periodic public reading of the treaty document which was deposited in the sanctuary of the vassal state. Deuteronomy xxxi. 9–13 provides for such a periodic reading of the law whilst the tradition that the Tables of the Law were deposited in the Ark (cf. Deut. x. 1–5) clearly parallels the placing of the Hittite treaty documents in the vassal's sanctuary.[1]

5. A fifth characteristic of these suzerainty treaties was the invocation of the deities of the vassals concerned as witnesses to the treaty. They usually also included the mountains, rivers, the heaven and the earth, the winds and clouds as witnesses. In Israel no 'gods', needless to say, are invoked. The nature of Israel's God clearly prohibited this. But it is interesting to note that now and again the prophets in inveighing against Israel's violation of the covenant call upon the heavens and the earth as Yahweh's witnesses. In Isaiah i.2 there is an appeal to the heavens and the earth whilst in Micah vi. 2 there is an appeal to the mountains and the 'foundations of the earth' (cf. also Deut. xxxii. 1; Jer. ii. 12). Similarly, in Deuteronomy iv. 26, xxx. 19, and xxxi. 28 Moses calls heaven and earth to serve as witnesses to any future breach of covenant by Israel. It is clear also from Joshua xxiv. 22 that Israel herself could be called as witness against her own disobedience: 'You are witnesses against yourselves that you have chosen the Lord, to serve him.'

6. Finally, the treaty concludes with a series of blessings and curses which will befall those who keep or violate the treaty obligations. In the Old Testament the Book of the Covenant, the law code in Deuteronomy, and the Holiness Code all conclude with such promises and threats (Exod. xxiii. 20f.; Deut. xxvii. 15f., xxviii; Lev. xxvi. 3 ff.).

Now it is clear from all this that in these old Hittite vassal treaties the historical retrospect—the parallel to the Old Testament credo theme—is an integral part of the covenant ceremony. In other words, we have here further evidence that the Old Testament cultic credo has its original *Sitz im Leben* precisely within the renewal of the covenant festival from which von Rad attempts to dissociate it. The pattern of this festival must therefore have been somewhat as follows:

1. Parenesis and exhortation together with a historical retrospect of Yahweh's saving deeds on Israel's behalf (*Heilsgeschichte* theme).

[1] Cf. G. E. Mendenhall, op. cit., pp. 64f., 66f.; W. Beyerlin, op. cit., pp. 55f.

2. The setting forth of the divine stipulations (Sinai covenant theme).
3. The making of a covenant.
4. The setting forth of blessings and curses.

Now a glance at the structure of Deuteronomy will reveal that it follows this pattern closely. Leaving aside those parts of the book which we have seen to be secondary additions, we have first of all the hortatory introduction (chs. v–xi) in which Israel is constantly reminded of her election and exhorted to obey the commandments of him who has so graciously chosen her to be his people. There follows the presentation of the divine laws which are to be observed by Israel (chs. xii–xxvi. 15). An actual covenant ceremony is presupposed by xxvi. 16–19 (cf. xxvii. 9–10). This is followed by the setting forth of the blessings which will befall Israel if she is faithful to the divine demands and the curses which will overtake her if she neglects them (ch. xxviii).

Accordingly, it may be concluded that the form in which Deuteronomy is cast derives from the cult and follows the liturgical pattern of the festival of the renewal of the covenant. The Deuteronomistic corpus itself bears witness in several places to the celebration of this festival. It is provided for in Deuteronomy xxxi. 9–13, whilst Joshua xxiv, as we have seen, is based upon it. At a later period Samuel officiates at such a festival at Gilgal (1 Sam. xii).[1] It is also probable that the so-called minor judges (Judges x. 1–5; xii. 7–15) exercised a similar function at the central shrine of the amphictyony. At least they seem to have been responsible for the maintenance of covenant law.[2]

Further striking evidence of the influence of the cult upon Deuteronomy comes from the repeated use of the phrase 'today' in the book. The frequent challenge and exhortation to serve and obey Yahweh 'this day' gains new significance if we see it as originating in this festival:[3]

> 'The Lord our God made a covenant with us in Horeb. The Lord made not this covenant with our fathers, but with us, even us, who are all of us here alive *this day*.'
>
> (Deut. v. 2–3)

'You shall remember the Lord your God, for it is he who gives you power

[1] Cf. J. Muilenburg, 'The form and structure of the covenantal formulations', *VT* 9 (1959), pp. 347–365.

[2] Cf. A. Alt, 'Die Ursprünge des israelitischen Rechts', *Kleine Schriften*, I (Munich, 1953), pp. 300f.; M. Noth, 'Das Amt des "Richters Israels" ', *Festschrift für Bertholet* (Tübingen, 1950), pp. 404ff.; G. von Rad, *Old Testament Theology*, I (1962), pp. 32f.

[3] Cf. G. von Rad, 'Das formgeschichtliche Problem des Hexateuch', op. cit., pp. 35f.

to get wealth; that he may confirm his covenant which he swore to your fathers, as at *this day*.'

(Deut. viii. 18)

'Behold, I set before you *this day* a blessing and a curse. . . .'

(Deut. xi. 26)

'And you shall be careful to do all the statutes and the ordinances which I set before you *this day*.'

(Deut. xi. 32)

'You have declared *this day* concerning the Lord that he is your God, and that you will walk in his ways, and keep his statutes and his commandments and his ordinances, and will obey his voice; and the Lord has declared *this day* concerning you that you are a people for his own possession, as he has promised you. . . .'

(Deut. xxvi. 17f.)

This brings us finally to a consideration of the peculiar homiletic style of Deuteronomy. The book is pervaded throughout with a sermon-like style which gives it its most pronounced characteristic. It is because of this that it is improper to conceive of Deuteronomy as primarily a legal code in which laws are formulated and punishments stipulated for failure to observe them. The really distinctive feature of the book is its urgent and appealing preaching style. The authors of Deuteronomy were concerned with driving home upon those who listen the only true motive for obedience—love of Yahweh. That is why it is in a very real sense true to say that the entire book is a commentary upon the command which stands at its beginning: 'You shall love the Lord your God with all your heart, and with all your soul, and with all your might' (Deut. vi. 5). The language of Deuteronomy is not, as W. Eichrodt has put it, that of the law but that of the heart and the conscience.[1] To quote further from the same writer:[2]

'Those who speak to us in the pages of Deuteronomy are men who know that a national law can never attain its goal so long as it remains a system reluctantly endured and effective only by compulsion; it must be founded on the inward assent of the people.'

The introduction in chapters v-xi comprises a series of exhortatory addresses which appeal again and again for faithfulness to the divine demands, whilst the laws themselves are also couched in this same parenetic language.[3] Such a presentation of the material in Deuteronomy displays a preaching technique which points for its origin to a

[1] W. Eichrodt, *Theology of the Old Testament*, I (London, 1961), p. 91. Cf. G. von Rad, *Studies in Deuteronomy*, p. 16.
[2] W. Eichrodt, *Theology of the Old Testament*, I, p. 91.
[3] Cf. G. von Rad, *Studies in Deuteronomy*, pp. 17f.

cultic milieu; it was, as one writer has put it, only after such a technique had been worked out in actual practice that it became a literary style in Deuteronomy.[1]

It is clear therefore that the cult has exercised a remarkable influence upon the form and manner of presentation of Deuteronomy. Whoever composed it stood within the cultic traditions of the old festival of the renewal of the covenant. We must see its peculiar homiletic style as deriving ultimately from this festival where in the course of the promulgation of the divine laws some cultic functionary was responsible for driving them home upon the minds and consciences of the congregation.

The vexed problem of the origin of Deuteronomy has been greatly illuminated in recent years by the complete transformation which has come about in our knowledge of the life and institutions of Israel in the pre-monarchical period. Older scholars generally agreed that the period of the Judges was ultimately of little significance in the development of the religion of the Old Testament. It was not until the advent of the monarchy that Israel attained any form of unity[2] and not until the great canonical prophets came on to the scene that the principles of lasting value, both ethical and theological, in the Old Testament came into being.[3]

Today this has all changed and this period is now viewed by the majority of scholars as the first great creative period in Israel's history. In America a school of thought closely associated with the name of W. F. Albright sees this as the period when the basic elements of Israel's faith deriving from the events of exodus and Sinai and centring on the figure of Moses were firmly established on the soil of Canaan and gave rise to certain theological and ethical norms which were to play a major role in Israel's history and in the development of her distinctive religion.[4] For the Alt-Noth school in Germany this was the period when the disparate traditions of

[1] G. von Rad, *Old Testament Theology*, I (1962), p. 72.

[2] The view of J. Wellhausen may be taken as typical (*Prolegomena to the History of Israel*, Edinburgh, 1885, p. 233): '. . . the regular constitution of the (Judges) period is the patriarchal anarchy of the system of families and septs . . . matters did not change until Israel became strong, that is to say, until his forces were welded into one by means of the monarchy'.

[3] On the older view of the innovations of the canonical prophets see further Wellhausen, ibid., pp. 473f. and for a critical assessment of this older view see R. E. Clements, *Prophecy and Covenant* (London, 1965), pp. 14ff.

[4] Cf. W. F. Albright, *From the Stone Age to Christianity*[2] (1946). Albright's basic position is followed and supported by such scholars as G. E. Wright, *The Old Testament against its Environment* (London, 1950), and *God who Acts* (London, 1952); J. Bright, *Early Israel in Recent History Writing* (London, 1956), and *A History of Israel* (London, 1960).

the various clans which, it is believed, went to make up Israel, were welded together and given their 'all Israel' orientation.[1]

Martin Noth has been largely responsible for our new understanding of the organization of Israel during the period of the Judges.[2] Noth points out that when we first meet Israel it is as a confederation of twelve tribes in the land of Canaan. These twelve tribes were not the result of an arbitrary or artificial splitting up of a greater whole but in fact represent a system of tribal organization which is witnessed to amongst other people and at other times.[3] The Greeks called such a tribal league an 'amphictyony' and Old Testament scholars have adopted this as a convenient term to designate the tribal organization of Israel in the pre-monarchical period.

Israel's tribal confederation was a theocratic community united in covenant with Yahweh. The name Israel, which may mean 'may God rule',[4] properly designates the Israelite amphictyony and its later use to designate northern Israel as distinct from Judah or Judah as distinct from northern Israel is purely secondary.[5] The focal point of the amphictyony was a central shrine where from time to time the tribes would assemble to worship and to discuss matters of mutual interest. It was at this central sanctuary that the festival of the renewal of the covenant of which we have already spoken must have taken place and at which the laws governing the covenant society were laid down and developed.[6] In the event of a breach of covenant law the tribes acted swiftly to punish the wrong-doer.[7] There was no standing army but when the life of the amphictyony was threatened the tribes rallied to its defence. It was part of the covenant obliga-

[1] Cf. A. Alt, 'Die Staatenbildung der Israliten in Palästina', *Kleine Schriften*, II (1953), pp. 1–65; M. Noth, *Das System der zwölf Stämme Israels*, *BWANT* IV:1 (Stuttgart, 1930); *Überlieferungsgeschichte des Pentateuch* (Stuttgart, 1948), and *The History of Israel*[2] (London, 1960), pp. 85ff. For a critical assessment of the Alt-Noth position see J. Bright, *Early Israel in Recent History Writing* (1956).

[2] M. Noth, *Das System der zwölf Stämme Israels* (1930) and *The History of Israel*[2] (1960), pp. 85ff.

[3] Cf. M. Noth, *The History of Israel*[2], p. 88.

[4] Cf. W. Eichrodt, *Theology of the Old Testament*, I (1961), p. 40 and note 7. For a discussion of the various interpretations of the name see G. A. Danell, *Studies in the Name Israel in the Old Testament* (Uppsala, 1946), pp. 15ff.

[5] Cf. M. Noth, *The History of Israel*[2], p. 3. See further G. A. Danell, op. cit., where it is shown that although in later times the name Israel was applied predominantly to the northern kingdom and occasionally to the Judaean state, it also retained among some circles its old sacral connotation as the name for 'all Israel'. Cf. also W. Beyerlin, *Die Kulttraditionen Israels in der Verkündigung des Propheten Micha*, *FRLANT* 54 (Göttingen, 1959), pp. 11ff.

[6] For the cultic origins of Israelite law cf. A. Alt, 'Die Ursprünge des israelitischen Rechts', *Kleine Schriften*, I (1953), pp. 278–332 where it is argued that the so-called apodeictic law had its origins in the cult of the amphictyonic period.

[7] Cf. M. Noth, *The History of Israel*[2], pp. 104f. The sexual offence against the wife of the levite recorded in Judges xix provides an example of such action.

tions that the clans should so rally for what was being fought was Yahweh's Holy War.[1] Those who did not respond to the call to arms were roundly cursed (cf. Judges v. 23; 1 Sam. xi. 7). Characteristic of the institution of the Holy War was what has been called charismatic leadership; the tribes were led into battle by one upon whom 'the spirit of Yahweh rushed' (cf. Judges iii. 10; xiv. 6; etc.). The notion of charismatic leadership, of leadership by divine designation and choice, was to play a vital role in Israel's history down through the centuries.[2]

Now a glance at the contents of Deuteronomy will reveal that the book stands within the traditions of this old Israelite amphictyony of the pre-monarchical period.[3] It was here that the festival of covenant renewal which has had such a remarkable influence upon Deuteronomy had its origins. It was celebrated periodically at the central shrine of the tribal league. One cannot avoid the feeling that this central shrine is the prototype, so to speak, of the Deuteronomic demand for the centralization of worship. The central shrine was, like the Deuteronomic 'place which Yahweh shall choose', the focal point of Israel's life. Nevertheless, it must always be borne in mind that Deuteronomy demands something much more radical by its law of the central shrine. In the amphictyony the central sanctuary did not exclude other local tribal shrines but in Deuteronomy these are prohibited. This more extreme demand for only one place of cultic worship for all Israel had its origin, as we shall see, at a much later time than the period of the tribal league.

The covenant which Deuteronomy seeks to renew is the covenant made between Yahweh and Israel on Horeb/Sinai and is based upon God's saving acts on Israel's behalf in the events of exodus and conquest. These are the sacral traditions upon which the covenant life of amphictyonic Israel was established. Deuteronomy affords no place to the later developments such as those centring on the covenant between Yahweh and the Davidic monarchy in Jerusalem. Indeed the law on kingship in Deuteronomy xvii. 14f. makes it quite clear that the authors of the book had little regard for the institution of monarchy. The expression 'like the nations that are round about' in verse 14 is itself polemical (cf. 1 Sam. viii. 5–9,

[1] On the Holy War see G. von Rad, *Der Heilige Krieg im alten Israel* (Göttingen, 1958), and *Studies in Deuteronomy*, pp. 45ff.

[2] Cf. J. Bright, *A History of Israel*, pp. 207, 211. Bright again and again points to the tenacity of the rule of charisma especially among prophetic circles in the northern kingdom.

[3] Cf. G. von Rad, *Studies in Deuteronomy*, p. 41; J. Bright, *A History of Israel*, pp. 299f.

19–20). For Deuteronomy kingship is essentially an institution of foreign importation. In this respect it occupies the same standpoint as the anti-monarchical narratives in 1 Samuel viii, xii. 6–25 which are now widely accepted as being based on old traditions rather than on later post-exilic 'retrospection'.[1]

But perhaps the strongest link between Deuteronomy and the traditions of the old tribal league is to be found in the amount of material in the book dealing with the sacral institutions of the Holy War. It is above all to von Rad that we owe this insight.[2] To begin with he points to the number of laws in Deuteronomy which deal specifically with war:

Deut. xx. 1–9: general laws concerning warfare.
Deut. xx. 10–20: laws concerning the besieging of cities.
Deut. xxi. 10–14: laws concerning female prisoners of war.
Deut. xxiii. 10–15 (EVV 9–14): rules concerning the military camp.
Deut. xxiv. 5: exemption from military service for newly married men.
Deut. xxv. 17–19: short statement concerning the hated Amalekite.

In addition to these laws von Rad has drawn attention to several speeches in the book which are saturated with the ideology of the Holy War. A good example is afforded in Deuteronomy vii. 16–26:[3]

> 'You shall destroy all the peoples that the Lord your God will give over to you, your eye shall not pity them; neither shall you serve their gods, for that would be a snare to you. If you shall say in your heart, "These nations are greater than I; how can I dispossess them?" you shall not be afraid of them, but you shall remember what the Lord your God did to Pharaoh and to all Egypt, the great trials which your eyes saw, the signs, the wonders, the mighty hand, and the outstretched arm, by which the Lord your God brought you out; so will the Lord your God do to all the peoples of whom you are afraid. Moreover the Lord your God will send a panic[4] among them, until those who are left and hide themselves from you are destroyed. You shall not be in dread of them; for the Lord your God is in the midst of you, a great and terrible God. The Lord your God will clear away these nations before you little by little. . . . But the Lord your God will give them over to you, and throw

[1] Cf. J. Bright, *A History of Israel*, p. 167 and the works referred to in footnote 10 on that page.
[2] Cf. von Rad, *Studies in Deuteronomy*, pp. 45ff. and *Der Heilige Krieg im alten Israel*, pp. 68ff.
[3] Cf. also Deut. ix. 1ff.; xi. 23; xxxi. 3f. See von Rad, *Studies in Deuteronomy*, pp. 51ff.
[4] For this rendering rather than the traditional 'hornet' see L. Köhler's note in *ZAW* 44 (1936), p. 291.

them into great confusion, until they are destroyed. And he will give their kings into your hand, and you shall make their name perish from under heaven; not a man shall be able to stand against you, until you have destroyed them. The graven images of their gods you shall burn with fire; you shall not covet the silver or the gold that is on them, or take it for yourselves, lest you be ensnared by it; for it is an abomination to the Lord your God. And you shall not bring an abominable thing into your house, and become accursed like it; you shall utterly detest and abhor it; for it is an accursed thing.'

Underlying this speech are the basic principles of the Holy War:[1] do not fear the hosts of the enemy for Yahweh himself is with you to fight for you, sending panic upon the enemy; but be careful not to take in booty anything under the sacred ban (חרם).

In addition to the laws and speeches dealing specifically with war, however, von Rad has shown the remarkable way in which the entire book is pervaded through and through with the ideology of the Holy War giving it a striking war-like atmosphere and militant spirit.[2] A few examples from those cited by him will serve to demonstrate this:

'And you shall do what is right and good in the sight of the Lord, that it may go well with you, and that you may go in and take possession of the good land which the Lord swore to give to your fathers by thrusting out all your enemies from before you, as the Lord has promised.'

(Deut. vi. 18f.)

'When the Lord your God brings you into the land which you are entering to take possession of it, and clears away many nations before you, the Hittites, the Girgashites, the Amorites, the Canaanites, the Perizzites, the Hivites, and the Jebusites, seven nations greater and mightier than yourselves, and when the Lord your God gives them over to you, and you defeat them; then you must utterly destroy them; you shall make no covenant with them, and show no mercy to them.'

(Deut. vii. 1ff.)

'When the Lord your God cuts off before you the nations whom you go in to dispossess, and you dispossess them and dwell in their land, take heed that you be not ensnared to follow them, after they have been destroyed before you, and that you do not enquire about their gods. . . .'

(Deut. xii. 29f.)

'When the Lord your God cuts off the nations whose land the Lord your God gives you, and you dispossess them and dwell in their cities and in their houses. . . .'

(Deut. xix. 1f.)

[1] Cf. G. von Rad, *Studies in Deuteronomy*, pp. 54f.

[2] Ibid., pp. 57ff.

'But in the cities of these peoples that the Lord your God gives you for an inheritance, you shall save alive nothing that breathes, but you shall utterly destroy them, the Hittites and the Amorites, the Canaanites and the Perizzites, the Hivites and the Jebusites, as the Lord your God has commanded. . . .'

(Deut. xx. 16f.)

In view of all this it may be concluded that Deuteronomy is firmly rooted in the sacral and cultic traditions of the old Israelite amphictyony of the pre-monarchical period. It has been pointed out, however, that we have in Deuteronomy no direct deposit of these old traditions. Deuteronomy itself made its appearance at a much later period than that of the tribal league and the old traditions with which it works have been modified and changed to suit the needs of a more advanced age in Israel's history. Thus, for example, the Israel to which Deuteronomy is addressed is already organized as a state and the older notion of individual autonomous tribes has well nigh faded.[1] Even in the matter of the Holy War there have been considerable modifications. In Deuteronomy the Holy Wars presuppose the functioning of military officials (שטרים) which came into being only after the establishment of the monarchy and the rise of a standing army.[2] Furthermore, Deuteronomy in contrast to the older period conceives the Holy War as offensive rather than defensive.[3] Again, the status of the central shrine is much more radically defined in Deuteronomy than in the amphictyonic period.[4] In addition, much of the legislation in the book has been formulated to deal with the needs of a relatively late period in Israel's history.[5]

If all this is granted then part of the problem of the provenance of Deuteronomy will be the question of where and by whom these old traditions were preserved and transmitted down through the centuries until their adaptation by the author of Deuteronomy. Whoever was responsible for the composition of the book evidently stood within the cultic and sacral traditions of the old Yahweh amphictyony of the period of the Judges.

There are yet, however, other distinct characteristics of Deuteronomy which must be accounted for in attempting to solve the problem of the origin of the book. Perhaps the most striking is the

[1] Cf. G. von Rad, *Old Testament Theology*, I (1962), p. 224.

[2] Cf. G. von Rad, ibid., p. 74 and *Der Heilige Krieg im alten Israel* (1958), p. 71 note 120.

[3] Cf. G. von Rad, *Der Heilige Krieg im alten Israel*, pp. 32, 70.

[4] Cf. M. Noth, *The History of Israel*[2] (1960), p. 276.

[5] Cf. M. Noth, *Exodus* (London, 1962), pp. 175ff.; H. Cazelles, *Etudes sur le Code de L'Alliance* (Paris, 1946), pp. 104ff.

Deuteronomic demand that all acts of cultic worship are to be carried out 'at the place which Yahweh shall choose'. Sacrifices and tithes are to be offered there (xii. 5, 11, 14, 18; xiv. 22f.; xv. 19f.); the Passover is to be observed only at 'the place' (xvi. 2, 5–6); this also applies to the feast of Weeks (xvi. 11) and Tabernacles (xvi. 15); all vows must be offered there (xv. 19f.; xxvi. 2); the juridical system is to have its 'arbitration' centre at the central shrine (xvii. 8). The book demands the destruction of all Yahweh sanctuaries other than this one (xii. 8–14). In demanding the centralization of the cult Deuteronomy is clearly an advancement upon the altar law in the Book of the Covenant in Exodus xx. 24 which reads:

> 'In every place where I cause my name to be remembered I will come unto you and bless you.'

This commonly accepted interpretation of the law of the sanctuary in Deuteronomy has been challenged by a number of scholars who argue that in fact the book demands nothing more in this respect than the altar law in Exodus xx. 24.[1] It is contended that both laws are aimed at prohibiting worship at shrines other than those specifically sanctioned by Yahweh. The Deuteronomic phrase (Deut. xii. 14) במקום אשר־יבחר יהוה באחד שבטיך is to be interpreted as follows: 'but in every place which Yahweh shall choose in any of your tribes'.[2] This translation is obtained by giving the definite article in במקום a distributive interpretation and the indefinite article in באחד a general meaning. It was attempted to justify this interpretation by drawing attention to the analogous use of the same words in the passage concerning the fugitive slave in Deuteronomy xxiii. 17 (EVV 16). Here it is legislated that the slave who escapes from his master is to be permitted to dwell במקום אשר־יבחר באחד שעריך. It was argued that the translation of this expression is clearly: 'he (the slave) shall dwell with you in any place which he shall choose within any of your gates'.[3] By the same token, it was concluded, the

[1] Cf. Th. Oestreicher, *Das Deuteronomische Grundgesetz* (Gütersloh, 1923); idem, 'Dtn. xii. 13f. im Licht von Dtn. xxiii. 16f.', *ZAW* 43 (1925), pp. 246–249; W. Staerk, *Das Problem des Deuteronomium* (Gütersloh, 1924), follows Oestreicher; A. C. Welch, *The Code of Deuteronomy: a new theory of its origin* (London, 1924); idem, 'The two descriptions of the sanctuary in Deuteronomy', *ExpT* 36 (1925), pp. 442–444 and *ExpT* 37 (1926), pp. 215–219; idem, 'The Problem of Deuteronomy', *JBL* 48 (1929), pp. 291–306; M. H. Segal, 'The Composition of the Pentateuch—a fresh examination', *Scripta Hierosolymitana*, vol. VIII (Jerusalem, 1961), p. 111.

[2] Cf. Th. Oestreicher, *Das Deuteronomische Grundgesetz*, p. 106.

[3] Cf. Th. Oestreicher, 'Dtn. xii. 13f. im Licht von Dtn. xxiii. 16f.', *ZAW* 43 (1925), pp. 246–249; A. C. Welch, *The Code of Deuteronomy*, pp. 48f.

expression concerning the sanctuary במקום אשר־יבחר יהוה באחד שבטיך is to be translated: 'in every place which Yahweh shall choose in any of your tribes'.

This argument has not, however, carried conviction.[1] In fact the law concerning the fugitive slave cannot be translated in this way. The correct translation can only be: 'he shall dwell with you in the place which he shall choose in one of your gates'. Since, however, the subject of this law clearly designates a *class* of people it is to be interpreted as meaning that runaway slaves are entitled to asylum in any Israelite town or village. But the sanctuary has Yahweh for its subject and therefore can only be translated and interpreted: 'in the place which Yahweh shall choose in one of your tribes'.[2] Besides, if the author had intended a multiplicity of Yahweh shrines to be legitimate places of worship, one would have expected him to have said just that by stating quite simply: 'but in the places (במקומות) which Yahweh shall choose in your tribes (בשבטיך)'.

Some scholars have expressed the opinion, however, that the demand for centralization in Deuteronomy can be removed easily from a literary critical point of view. Thus von Rad states:[3] 'It is being increasingly recognized that the demand for centralization in Deuteronomy rests upon a very narrow basis only, and is, from the point of view of literary criticism, comparatively easy to remove as a late and final adaptation of many layers of material'.

If by this it is believed that the centralization demand is among the later cultic developments in Israel taken up by the author of Deuteronomy, then there can be no grounds for disagreement. But if it is suggested that the demand can be excised from the present book as a later interpolation, then this can hardly be upheld. The demand occurs again and again in the course of the book. Not only, however, is there this insistence on centralization; there are in Deuteronomy various provisions which are the direct result of the abolition of the local sanctuaries. Thus, since the slaughtering of animals for domestic use had hitherto been a sacrificial act carried out at the local altars, the difficulty now arose as to how this was to be performed if all these local altars were abolished. Hence the law in Deuteronomy

[1] Cf. E. König, 'Der generelle Artikel im Hebräischen', *ZAW* 44 (1926), pp. 173f.; idem, 'Stimmen Exod. xx. 24 und Deut. xii. 13f. zusammen?' *ZAW* 42 (1924), pp. 347f.; A. R. Siebens, *L'Origine du Code Deutéronomique* (Paris, 1929), pp. 108f.

[2] Cf. E. König, 'Der generelle Artikel im Hebräischen', *ZAW* 44, p. 173; A. R. Siebens, op. cit., p. 109.

[3] G. von Rad, *Studies in Deuteronomy*, p. 67. Cf. V. Maag, 'Erwägungen zur deuteronomischen Kultzentralisation', *VT* 6 (1956), p. 10.

xii. 20–25 (cf. xiv. 22–26) which permits the 'profane' slaughter of animals for domestic use. Again, since the abolition of the local shrines will deprive their priestly personnel of their livelihood, it is legislated that they are to be permitted to minister at the central sanctuary if they so desire (xviii. 6–8). It is probable also that the abolition of the local altars with its consequences for these priests is the reason for the constant commendation of their needs to the people (Deut. xii. 12, 18, 19; xiv. 27, 29; xvi. 11, 14; xxvi. 11, 12, 13). Furthermore, the centralization of the cult led to a corresponding centralization of the juridical rights of the priesthood (cf. xvii. 8f.). All this is surely sufficient evidence that the demand for centralization by no means rests upon a narrow basis. In fact, far from being easily removed from the point of view of literary criticism, it would require nothing less than violent surgery of the text to remove the centralization demand with all its consequences and associated laws from the book. It belongs without any doubt to the original composition of the book of Deuteronomy and must therefore be seen as having been an essential part of the author's theology. It is integral to the very character of the book. The total demand which Deuteronomy makes has often been summed up in the apt German phrase *ein Gott*, *ein Volk*, *ein Kult*. The demand for *Kultuseinheit* is wholly in keeping with the demand that Israel as *ein Volk* should worship *ein Gott*. On both literary and theological grounds therefore the demand for centralization must be considered a basic feature of Deuteronomy. In the discussion of the origin and authorship of the book it must, accordingly, be accounted for.

It is in connection with the law of the centralization of worship that we meet with yet another theological characteristic of Deuteronomy, viz. the Deuteronomic concept of the nature of Yahweh's dwelling among his people.[1] To the question of where Israel is to have communion with her God Deuteronomy gives this answer: Yahweh will choose out a place where he will 'make his name dwell' (cf. Deut. xii. 5, 11, etc.). It has been rightly pointed out that the notion of the 'name' as the form of Yahweh's manifestation is not itself unique in Deuteronomy. Already at an earlier period the Book of the Covenant conceived of Yahweh's sanctuaries as the places where he has caused his name to be recorded (cf. Exod. xx. 24).[2] What is new in Deuteronomy, however, is the radical definition of this concept whereby not Yahweh himself but his name is present in the

[1] Cf. G. von Rad, *Studies in Deuteronomy*, pp. 37ff.
[2] Cf. G. von Rad, op. cit., p. 38.

sanctuary. In other words, Deuteronomy is concerned with emphasizing the distance between God and the sanctuary and in so doing is attempting to replace, as von Rad has put it, the old crude idea of Yahweh's presence and dwelling at the shrine by a theologically sublimated idea.[1] Yahweh cannot be contained in a temple—heaven and the highest heaven cannot contain him (cf. 1 Kings viii. 27f.). We have already observed the influence of this name-theology upon the Deuteronomistic concept of the Ark. It is, as we have seen, highly probable that the original book nowhere mentioned the Ark and it can only be concluded that the old notion of the Ark as the throne of the invisibly present Yahweh had faded among the circles responsible for the Deuteronomic traditions and had been replaced by the loftier theologumenon of the name of Yahweh as the manner of his manifestation in the sanctuary. This is further evidenced by the fact that when the Ark came within the orbit of the Deuteronomic traditions it was regarded only as the receptacle for the tables of the law.[2]

Yet another characteristic of Deuteronomy is its definition of the relationship between Yahweh and Israel in terms of election. We have already stressed that underlying the book is the old Sinai covenant tradition with its twofold aspect of Yahweh's redemption of Israel from bondage and the obligations which this placed upon Israel. The covenant at Sinai was seen to establish formally the relationship between Yahweh and Israel brought about by the deliverance from Egypt. Right from the beginning, therefore, Israel believed herself as standing in a unique relationship to Yahweh, as being, in fact, his peculiar people. In emphasizing this bond between Yahweh and Israel with all the responsibilities it entailed for Israel, Deuteronomy is therefore heir to a concept as old as Israel herself. What is new in Deuteronomy, however, is its distinctive use of the verb *bāḥar* 'choose' to define Yahweh's action on Israel's behalf in history.[3] In other words, as far as the Old Testament literature is concerned, the doctrine of Yahweh's election of Israel to be his people, though implied in Israel's faith from the beginning is first defined in Deuteronomy:[4]

[1] G. von Rad, op. cit., p. 39. Cf. Th. C. Vriezen, *An Outline of Old Testament Theology* (Oxford, 1958), pp. 248f.

[2] Cf. G. von Rad, *Studies in Deuteronomy*, pp. 39f.; F. Dumermuth, op. cit., pp. 70ff.

[3] Cf. G. von Rad, *Das Gottesvolk im Deuteronomium*, *BWANT* III:2 (Stuttgart, 1929), p. 28; Th. C. Vriezen, *Die Erwählung Israels nach dem Alten Testament* (Zürich, 1953), p. 47; G. E. Mendenhall, 'Election', *IDB*, II (1962), pp. 76f.

[4] Cf. G. von Rad, *Old Testament Theology*, I (1962), p. 178.

'For you are a people holy to the Lord your God; the Lord your God has chosen you to be a people for his own possession, out of all the peoples that are on the face of the earth.'

(Deut. vii. 6)

Here then we have yet another distinctive feature of Deuteronomy which must be accounted for in the discussion of the provenance and authorship of the book. What is the background of this Deuteronomic formulation of the doctrine of election?

This survey of the nature of Deuteronomy and its dominant characteristics helps to set in relief the problem of the provenance and authorship of the book and supplies us with definite leads for our discussion of this question. We have observed the cultic background to the book and the striking influence which the old festival of the renewal of the covenant has exercised upon it in both form and presentation. In addition, it has been established that in its broad basis Deuteronomy stands within the sacral traditions of the old Israelite amphictyony. This was particularly evidenced by the amount of material in the book which has its basis in the ideology of the Holy War. At the same time it has become clear that Deuteronomy contains no direct deposit of the institutions of this old amphictyony. The material in the book betrays modifications and developments which could have arisen only at a time much in advance of the period of the tribal league. This is particularly obvious, as we have noted, in the case of the material dealing with the Holy War. But it is even more in evidence in Deuteronomy's spiritually exalted name-theology and in its distinctive definition of the doctrine of election. Finally, and not least of all, the demand for the centralization of the cult must certainly have originated at a relatively late period in Israel's history.

The question now becomes one of deciding where and by what circles these traditions and principles were preserved down through the centuries until they finally made their appearance in the form of Deuteronomy.

CHAPTER IV

DEUTERONOMY AND NORTHERN ISRAEL

In recent years an increasing number of scholars have accepted and supported the theory that Deuteronomy derives either directly or ultimately from northern Israel where, it is believed, the old amphictyonic traditions upon which it is based were preserved and transmitted down through the centuries.[1] The older theory that Deuteronomy with its demand for the centralization of the cult was drawn up in the interests of the Jerusalem Temple and therefore by a pro-Jerusalem circle if not the Jerusalem priesthood itself has been almost totally rejected. The most extreme presentation of the theory of the northern origin of the book comes from A. Alt who sees in it a restoration programme drawn up in northern Israel sometime after the catastrophe of 721 B.C.[2] For Alt it was composed in the north, by northern circles for the north; how it came to be in the Jerusalem Temple in Josiah's reign is a mystery we shall never solve.[3] Others take a less radical position in the matter. A. Weiser, for example, agrees with Alt that Deuteronomy is a restoration programme drawn up in the north but suggests that circles of Judaean cultic prophets

[1] Cf. C. F. Burney, *The Book of Judges* (London, 1918), p. xlvi footnote; A. C. Welch, *The Code of Deuteronomy: a new theory of its origin* (London, 1924), and *Deuteronomy: the framework to the Code* (London, 1932); A. Bentzen, *Die josianische Reform und ihre Voraussetzungen* (Copenhagen, 1926); F. Horst, *Das Privilegrecht Jahves* (*FRLANT* 45, N.F. 28, 1930), now in his *Gesammelte Studien* (Munich, 1961), pp. 17–154; J. Hempel, *Die Althebräische Literatur* (Wildpark-Potsdam, 1930–34), pp. 126, 139; W. F. Albright, *From the Stone Age to Christianity*[2] (1946), p. 241; G. A. Danell, *Studies in the Name Israel in the Old Testament* (Uppsala, 1946), pp. 53f.; I. Engnell, *Symbolae Biblicae Uppsalienses*, vii (1946), pp. 21f.; H. Cazelles, *Introduction à la Bible* (ed. A. Robert and A. Feuillet, Paris, 1953), and *Le Deutéronome* (Paris, 1958); A. Alt, 'Die Heimat des Deuteronomiums', *Kleine Schriften*, II (1953), pp. 250–275; G. E. Wright, *Deuteronomy, IB*, II (1953), pp. 311–330; J. Bowman, 'The Samaritans and the Book of Deuteronomy', *TGUOS* 17 (1958), pp. 9–18; F. Dumermuth, 'Zur deuteronomischen Kulttheologie und ihre Voraussetzungen', *ZAW* 70 (1958), pp. 59–98; B. W. Anderson, *The Living World of the Old Testament* (1958), pp. 311–312; J. Bright, *A History of Israel* (1960), pp. 299–300; A. Weiser, *Introduction to the Old Testament* (1961), p. 132; G. Henton Davies, *Peake's Commentary*[2] (1962), p. 269; J. A. Bewer, *The Literature of the Old Testament*[3] (revised by E. G. Kraeling, London, 1962), p. 126; H. Ringgren, *Israelitische Religion* (Stuttgart, 1963), p. 150; N. W. Porteous, 'Actualization and the Prophetic Criticism of the Cult', *Tradition und Situation: Studien zur alttestamentliche Prophetie* (Festschrift für A. Weiser, ed. E. Würthwein and O. Kaiser, Göttingen, 1963), pp. 99f.

[2] A. Alt, 'Die Heimat des Deuteronomiums', *Kleine Schriften*, II (1953), pp. 250f.

[3] Ibid., p. 275.

cherished and preserved it after the destruction of the northern kingdom.[1] Others, like J. Bright, whilst agreeing that the traditions underlying Deuteronomy are from northern Israel, suggest that they were brought south to Judah sometime after 721 B.C. and there reformulated into a programme of reform.[2]

In this chapter and in the next we shall be concerned with the problem of the origin and authorship of Deuteronomy. Here we shall deal with the case for the north Israelite origin of the book. In the next chapter we shall have to examine the relationship between the book and Judah.

The currently widely accepted theory of the north Israelite provenance of Deuteronomy has its beginnings in the work of A. C. Welch in the 1920s.[3] In a series of publications on the matter Welch broke radically with the dominant theory of that period concerning the problem of Deuteronomy. In the first place, he argued that the book was composed in the tenth century and not, as commonly agreed, in the seventh.[4] In the second place, he contended that except for the law formulated in Deuteronomy xii. 1–7, regarded by him as secondary, the original book nowhere demands the centralization of the cult.[5] And thirdly, he argued that the book originated in northern Israel.[6]

Of these three points neither of the first two has carried conviction. The majority of scholars still accept the seventh-century date for the actual composition of the book whilst acknowledging, as we have seen, that it is based upon very ancient traditions and material. The argument that the centralization of worship is nowhere demanded in Deuteronomy has been almost totally rejected.[7] Welch's third suggestion, however, viz. that Deuteronomy originated in northern Israel, has been widely supported in recent years.

Welch saw evidence of the northern origin of the book at several points. Like other commentators before and after him, he emphasized the connections between Deuteronomy and Hosea but argued at the same time that the former influenced the latter and not, as usually held, the latter the former.[8] He believed too that the law of kingship

[1] A. Weiser, *Introduction to the Old Testament* (1961), p. 132.
[2] J. Bright, *A History of Israel* (1960), pp. 299f.
[3] Welch's views are presented mainly in his *The Code of Deuteronomy* (1924). Cf. also his later *Deuteronomy: the framework to the Code* (1932).
[4] A. C. Welch, *The Code of Deuteronomy*, pp. 206ff.
[5] Ibid., pp. 46f.
[6] Ibid., pp. 38f., 74f., 113, 128f.
[7] See above pp. 53f.
[8] A. C. Welch, *The Code of Deuteronomy*, pp. 32f. Cf. A. Alt, 'Die Heimat des Deuteronomiums', op. cit., pp. 266f.

in Deuteronomy xvii. 14f. is northern in its attitude and again found resemblances between it and Hosea's attitude.[1] Again like other scholars, Welch pointed to the literary parallels between Deuteronomy and the Elohist document in the Pentateuch.[2] He contended further that the Passover law in Deuteronomy xvi. 1–8 belongs to the same (northern) stream of tradition from which the later Samaritan practice sprang.[3] Finally, Welch suggested that the law of the tithe which occurs frequently in the book (xii. 6, 11, 17; xiv. 22, 23, 28; xxvi. 12) may have had its origin at the sanctuary of Bethel.[4] It was then argued that this northern book together with other northern literature and traditions found its way to Judah at the time of the Josianic reformation.[5]

The arguments adduced more recently for the northern origin of Deuteronomy are in part the same as those advanced by Welch and in part quite different. The differences are due for the most part to the new understanding which has come about concerning the broad traditional basis upon which the book stands—the traditions of the old Israelite amphictyony—as well as the new insights into the important role played by the cult in the formation of the literature of the Old Testament. We have already drawn attention to the extraordinary influence of the old festival of the renewal of the covenant upon the form and presentation of Deuteronomy and it is here that we may begin our survey of the more recent discussion concerning the provenance of the book.

During the period of the tribal league the traditions seem to have had their home at the central shrine where the covenant festival was celebrated from time to time, very probably annually in the autumn. In the earliest period this seems to have been at Shechem.[6] The Deuteronomistic literature itself bears evidence of this. The narrative of what has been called 'the diet of Shechem' in Joshua xxiv points in this direction. We have already seen that Joshua's speech to the assembly gathered at this old sanctuary follows the pattern of the

[1] A. C. Welch, *The Code of Deuteronomy*, pp. 117f.; cf. A. Alt, 'Die Heimat des Deuteronomiums', op. cit., pp. 271f.

[2] A. C. Welch, *The Code of Deuteronomy*, pp. 113f. Cf. G. E. Wright, *Deuteronomy*, *IB*, II, (1953), p. 318.

[3] A. C. Welch, *The Code of Deuteronomy*, pp. 74f. and his article 'On the method of celebrating Passover', *ZAW* 45 (1927), pp. 24–29. Cf. J. Bowman, 'The Samaritans and the Book of Deuteronomy', *TGUOS* 17 (1958), pp. 9–18.

[4] A. C. Welch, *The Code of Deuteronomy*, pp. 38f.

[5] A. C. Welch, *Deuteronomy: the framework to the Code* (1932), p. 205. Cf. also his article 'When was the worship of Israel centralized to the Temple?', *ZAW* 43 (1925), pp. 250f.

[6] Cf. M. Noth, *The History of Israel*[2] (1960), pp. 91f.

covenant festival. In addition, the Deuteronomistic passages (Deut. xi. 29f.; xxvii; Joshua viii. 30–35) which record that after the conquest the tribes built an altar near Shechem and set up twelve stones upon which the law was inscribed and proclaimed blessings and curses probably have this same festival as their background.[1] It is possible also that at a slightly later period the central shrine was located for at least a short time at Gilgal[2] and Bethel[3] so that the old traditions would have also attached themselves to these cultic centres.

For most of the amphictyonic period, however, the central sanctuary seems to have been located at Shiloh and it was there when the tribal league broke up under the pressure of the Philistines (I Sam. iv). Here there was evidently a temple in which the Ark, the sacred cultic object of the twelve tribes, was housed (cf. I Sam. iii. 3; Jer. vii. 14, xxvi. 9). In the case of Shiloh there is strong evidence that here also a covenant festival was held annually in the autumn. Judges xxi. 19 'Behold, there is a yearly feast of the Lord at Shiloh' may be a reference to it. It is also noted in I Samuel i. 3 that Elkanah, Samuel's father, went up to Shiloh from year to year 'to worship and to sacrifice to the Lord of hosts'.[4] Samuel's close connections with Shiloh also point in this direction since, as we shall see presently, he represented strongly the amphictyonic traditions.

It may be concluded therefore that for the period of the Judges the traditions had their home in the central shrine of the twelve-tribe confederation where the tribes gathered periodically to renew the covenant with Yahweh their God. The sacral traditions and observances which had become associated with the various central sanctuaries of the amphictyony probably continued to be preserved even after the Ark had been removed to a new location. Hence even after they ceased to be the central shrine of the tribal league it is very probable that Shechem, Bethel and Gilgal remained centres of the covenant traditions.[5]

The question now arises as to where the traditions were preserved after the collapse of the amphictyony. Shiloh was destroyed by the Philistines about 1050 B.C. and evidently fell into the background (cf. I Sam. iv; Jer. vii. 12, 14, xxvi. 6, 9).[6] Samuel seems to have

[1] Ibid., p. 92.

[2] Ibid., p. 95.

[3] Ibid., pp. 94f. Cf. A. Alt, 'Die Wallfahrt von Sichem nach Bethel', *Kleine Schriften*, I (1953), pp. 79ff.

[4] Cf. M. Noth, *The History of Israel*[2] pp. 97f.; W. McKane, *I and II Samuel* (London, 1963), p. 35.

[5] Cf. M. Noth, *The History of Israel*[2], pp. 92f.

[6] The Danish excavations in 1926 unearthed evidence of the destruction of Shiloh in about 1050 B.C. See H. Kjaer, 'The Danish Excavation of Shiloh', *PEQ* 59 (1927), pp. 202–213.

moved away from it. On the other hand, it is noteworthy that at a much later period Ahijah, who designated Jeroboam I to be first king of the breakaway northern tribes and who almost certainly represented the old amphictyonic principles,[1] came from Shiloh and it is not unreasonable to suppose that he may have been at the head of a prophetic circle still operating at the old tribal centre.[2] It is clear also that in spite of the collapse of the amphictyony both Bethel and Gilgal remained important cult centres for Israel. Gilgal indeed appears to have risen again to a position of importance and figures prominently in the activities of Samuel (1 Sam. vii. 16; x. 8; xi. 14, 15; xv. 21). It has been plausibly suggested recently that Gilgal was the scene of a covenant ceremony which marked the end of the old amphictyonic order and the beginning of the new with the coming of monarchy under Saul (1 Sam. xi. 14–xii).[3] Bethel too seems to have been of significance (1 Sam. vii. 16; x. 3). Both Gilgal and Bethel were included in Samuel's itinerary and in 1 Samuel vii. 16 it is recorded that he 'judged Israel' at these places. It is significant that this same expression is employed to designate the function of the so-called 'minor judges' in Judges x. 1–5; xii. 7–15. It has been shown that these functionaries were officials of the tribal league who were responsible for the administration of covenant law.[4] In view of this it is reasonable to conclude that at both Gilgal and Bethel Samuel administered covenant law after the analogy of these judges in whose succession he evidently stood.[5] Shechem was the scene of an early attempt at kingship in Israel and Abimelech is said to have reigned there as king for three years (Judges ix. 22). This short-lived monarchy, however, led ultimately to the destruction of the city at the hands of Abimelech himself (Judges ix. 45f.).[6] In spite of this Shechem retained its prestige. Rehoboam went up to it where 'all Israel' was gathered to make him king (1 Kings xii)

[1] Cf. J. Bright, *A History of Israel*, p. 211.

[2] Bright suggests (op. cit., p. 218 n. 32) that Ahijah may have desired a restoration of the amphictyonic cult at Shiloh. On the other hand, Noth ('Jerusalem und die israelitische Tradition', *Gesammelte Studien*, Munich, 1960, pp. 172ff.) argues that Ahijah's final break with Jeroboam was because he (Ahijah) approved political but not cultic separation from Jerusalem.

[3] Cf. J. Muilenburg, 'The form and structure of the covenantal formulations', *VT* 9 (1959), pp. 347–365.

[4] Cf. A. Alt, 'Die Ursprünge des israelitischen Rechts', *Kleine Schriften*, I (1953), pp. 300f.; M. Noth, *The History of Israel*², pp. 101f. and 'Das Amt des "Richters Israels" ', *Festschrift Alfred Bertholet* (Tübingen, 1950), pp. 404–417; W. McKane, op. cit., pp. 63f.

[5] Cf. J. Bright, op. cit., p. 166; W. McKane, op. cit., pp. 63f.

[6] For archaeological evidence of this see E. F. Campbell and J. F. Ross, 'The Excavation of Shechem and the Biblical Tradition', *BA* 26 (1963), no. 1 p. 17.

and when he refused to meet the demands of the northern tribes it became the centre of the revolution and secession of these tribes under Jeroboam (1 Kings xii. 16f.). After this Shechem became for a time the capital of the breakaway kingdom but thereafter is little mentioned.

It is very probable therefore that these old amphictyonic shrines continued to preserve and transmit the covenant traditions even after the amphictyony proper had been broken up by the Philistines. That this situation continued for some time seems clear, for at a later period Bethel was still evidently the centre of a prophetic circle and both Elijah and Elisha apparently frequented it (2 Kings ii. 2, 3). This is true also of Gilgal (2 Kings ii. 1; iv. 38).

Before long, however, the cultic transmission of the covenant faith at these sanctuaries seems to have collapsed. Bethel and Gilgal are condemned in the mid-eighth century by both Amos and Hosea:

> 'Come to Bethel, and transgress;
> to Gilgal, and multiply transgression;
> bring your sacrifices every morning,
> your tithes every three days;
> offer a sacrifice of thanksgiving of
> that which is leavened,
> and proclaim freewill offerings,
> publish them;
> for so you love to do, O people of Israel!'
> (Amos iv. 4–5)

> 'For thus says the Lord to the house of Israel:
> "Seek me and live;
> but do not seek Bethel,
> and do not enter into Gilgal
> or cross over to Beer-sheba;
> for Gilgal shall surely go into exile,
> and Bethel shall come to nought."'
> (Amos v. 4–5)

And from the same period comes Hosea's similar invective against both Gilgal and Bethel (Bethaven!) (Hos. iv. 15; ix. 15; x. 5, 15;[1] xii. 12, EVV 11). It is possible too that Hosea vi. 9 is to be taken as indicating that Shechem also had been corrupted by its priesthood who are here branded as brigands and murderers.[2] In fact the total

[1] Cf. LXX which reads Bethel for the MT 'House of Israel'.

[2] The text is corrupt. E. Nielsen, *Shechem*[2] (1959), p. 290, accepts in part J. Pedersen's reconstruction (*Israel: Its Life and Culture III–IV*, 1940, p. 171), and

picture conveyed by the oracles of Hosea and Amos is that the covenant faith with its emphasis upon Yahweh's grace towards Israel and the divine demands was at fading point or even totally absent in the life of the Israelite society of their day:

> 'There is no faithfulness or kindness, and no
> knowledge of God in the land;
> there is swearing, lying, killing, stealing,
> and committing adultery;
> they break all bounds and murder follows murder.'
> (Hos. iv. 1f. Cf. Amos ii. 6f.; v. 12f.)

And those held most responsible for this state of affairs are, as far as Hosea is concerned, the priests (Hos. iv. 4f); they have ceased to teach and promulgate the covenant faith in Israel so that the people are 'destroyed for lack of knowledge' (Hos. iv. 6).[1] Hand in hand with the failure of the priesthood has come the failure of the cult. In times past the centres of covenant life where the knowledge and will of Yahweh were perennially made known to Israel, the great

[1] H. W. Wolff, '"Wissen um Gott" bei Hosea als Urform von Theologie', *EvTh* 12 (1952–53), pp. 533–554 now in his *Gesammelte Studien*, 1964, pp. 182ff. has argued that the expression 'knowledge of God' in Hosea designates specifically a knowledge of the Sinai covenant with its twofold aspect of salvation history and covenant law. Against this it has been argued that the expression in Hosea is paralleled by such words as 'steadfast love' (חסד) and 'faithfulness' (אמת) (Hos. iv. 1; vi. 6) and may therefore connotate nothing more than the moral and ethical content of these words. Cf. N. W. Porteous, 'Actualization and the Prophetic Criticism of the Cult', *Tradition und Situation* (ed. E. Würthwein and O. Kaiser, 1963), p. 97. Cf. J. L. McKenzie, 'Knowledge of God in Hosea', *JBL* 74 (1955), pp. 22f.

partly H. S. Nyberg's suggestion (*Studien zum Hoseabuche* (Uppsala, 1935), pp. 42f.) and renders:

> 'As robbers lie in wait,
> a gang of priests
> along the road they murder unto Shechem,
> yea, wicked plans they carry out.'

Nielsen then concludes (op. cit., p. 323) that this is no condemnation of Shechem and its cult. H. W. Wolff, who believes that Shechem was the centre of a circle of faithful levites, suggests that this verse may have as its background the opposition of the official priesthood to this circle (cf. his 'Hoseas geistige Heimat', *Gesammelte Studien*, Munich, 1964, p. 249 n. 70). A. Weiser, *Das Buch der zwölf kleinen Propheten I* (*ATD* 24, Göttingen, 1949), suggests that the background to Hosea vi. 7–11 was a cultic pilgrimage from east Jordan to Shechem. On the other hand more consideration should be given to G. R. Driver's suggestion ('Notes and Studies', *JTS* 39, 1938, p. 156) that דֶּרֶךְ should be emended to דָּרְכוּ to read: 'they sally forth, they murder at Shechem'. (Cf. J. Mauchline, *Hosea*, *IB*, VI, 1956, p. 630.) This then would be a condemnation of the priesthood at Shechem itself. Cf. further N. W. Porteous, 'The Prophets and the Problem of Continuity', *Israel's Prophetic Heritage* (ed. B. W. Anderson and W. Harrelson, London, 1962) p. 16 and his 'Actualization and the Prophetic Criticism of the Cult', *Tradition und Situation* (ed. E. Würthwein and O. Kaiser, 1963), p. 100.

sanctuaries together with the local shrines were now the scene of Canaanite pagan cults and rites of the grossest nature (cf. Hos. ii. 15, EVV. 13; iv. 11f.; Amos ii. 7). The religiosity of the day, the endless sacrifices, the festivals and solemn occasions, were condemned outright as no substitute for the observance of Yahweh's covenant demands:

> 'I hate, I despise your feasts,
> and I take no delight in your solemn assemblies.
> Even though you offer me your burnt offerings and
> cereal offerings,
> I will not accept them,
> and the peace offerings of your fatted beasts
> I will not look upon.
> Take away from me the noise of your songs:
> to the melody of your harps I will not listen.
> But let justice roll down like waters,
> and righteousness like an ever-flowing stream.'
> (Amos v. 21–24)

> 'For I desire steadfast love and not sacrifice,
> the knowledge of God, rather than burnt offerings.'
> (Hos. vi. 6)

It is clear therefore that by the time of Amos and Hosea the cult had ceased to preserve and promulgate Israel's covenant faith. This then raises the problem of by what means or by whom the covenant traditions were cherished and transmitted through such periods of apostasy as that which formed the background to the preaching of these two prophets.

The evidence suggests that it is above all to the prophetic party that we are to look for the custodians of the old traditions.[1] After the destruction of the amphictyony it was to the figure of Samuel and the associated prophetic guilds that the covenant faith owed its survival and we have already drawn attention to the connection of the prophetic party with the great cult centres during the early monarchy. From the beginning of his life Samuel had been closely connected with the amphictyonic shrine of Shiloh and there are strong grounds for believing that he stood in the succession of the amphictyonic judges. We can be sure that he was steeped in the sacral traditions of the tribal league and strove to keep them alive during the dark days

[1] For this see N. W. Porteous, 'The Prophets and the Problem of Continuity', *Israel's Prophetic Heritage* (ed. B. W. Anderson and W. Harrelson, London, 1962), pp. 11–25.

of Philistine dominion when amphictyonic life had broken down and the faith was struggling for its survival. Samuel's loyalty to the old traditions is perhaps best seen in his clash with the new monarchical order under Saul. It is very probable that he was suspicious of the monarchy right from the beginning. It is being increasingly recognized that the narrative in 1 Samuel viii, x. 17f., xii which records Samuel's opposition to the institution of kingship is not a later retrospection, as some older scholars believed,[1] but quite possibly reflects the reaction of the representatives of the old order to an institution which they regarded as foreign and as constituting a definite threat to covenantal traditions and practices.[2] This attitude is typified in the reply of Gideon to the request that he should become king:

> 'Gideon said to them: I will not rule over you, and my son will not rule over you; the Lord will rule over you.'
>
> (Judges viii. 23)

Yahweh was king of the covenant society of amphictyonic Israel (cf. Judges ix. 7 ff.; 1 Sam. xii. 12). Samuel himself was quick to condemn any attempt of the monarchy to violate any of the traditions and practices of the tribal league. Thus, for example, in 1 Samuel xiii. 4b–15 he accuses Saul of attempting to usurp the functions of the amphictyonic priesthood and in chapter xv he condemns him for having violated the Holy War laws of the ban (חרם). Finally, it is significant that Samuel's opposition led to the rejection of Saul (cf. 1 Sam. xv. 23, 26).

This concern of the prophetic party for the old traditions continued down through the centuries. Northern Israel was evidently the scene of their most vigorous activity. There were probably several reasons for this. The challenge of the Canaanite religion was stronger in the north where the nature of the country lent itself to the agricultural pursuits with which much of the worship of Baal was associated. The south was for the most part more suited to the ancestral shepherd life and was less exposed to the danger of syncretism although, as we shall see, by no means free from it. Furthermore, the north was altogether more cosmopolitan than the south. The main concentration of population was in the north and the country was, unlike Judah, more open to both the religious and cultural influence of foreign peoples, particularly Phoenicia and Syria. It must be borne in mind

[1] Cf. J. Wellhausen, *Prolegomena to the History of Israel* (Edinburgh, 1885), pp. 254f.

[2] Cf. J. Bright, op. cit., p. 167; W. McKane, op. cit., p. 67; J. Pedersen, op. cit., p. 99.

also that the old tribal league had had its focal points in northern sanctuaries (Shechem, Gilgal, Bethel and Shiloh); it was not until the time of David that Judah began to play a prominent role. To what extent the traditions were kept alive in the south will be considered later.

The tenacity of the amphictyonic traditions in the north is perhaps most in evidence in the clash between the prophetic circles there and the monarchy. We have already observed Samuel's resentment of Saul's violation of the old traditions and practices, and his successors continued to keep a watchful eye on the activity of the monarchy.

The disruption can be explained as being for the most part the reaction of those loyal to the old traditions to Solomon's oppressive measures and the state's encroachments upon the ancient prerogatives of tribal life and its disregard for covenant law. It is significant that it was a prophet, Ahijah, who led the revolt against the House of David and designated Jeroboam as king of the breakaway tribes (1 Kings xi. 29f.). It is probable too that Ahijah and his followers resented the state's annexation of the amphictyonic shrine and its consequent control over it.[1] Such resentment was undoubtedly augmented by the pagan influence brought to Jerusalem by Solomon's marriage-alliances with foreign powers (1 Kings xi. 1f.). We must also see in Ahijah's designation of Jeroboam as king the refusal of the representatives of the old order to accept the principle of dynastic succession and the tenacity of the charismatic principle so characteristic of the amphictyonic period. This indeed is further evidenced by the fact that the north never succeeded in maintaining a stable dynasty. Jeroboam I, himself designated as king by a prophet, was rejected by that same prophet (1 Kings xiv. 7f.). Similarly, Baasha who exterminated the house of Jeroboam (1 Kings xv. 27f.) was also apparently raised to power by prophetic designation and rejected by the prophets (1 Kings xvi. 1–7).

The prophets too were responsible for the revolution which raised Jehu to the throne (2 Kings ix. 1–10) and brought the house of Omri to its long-remembered bloody end (2 Kings ix. 30–x. 11; cf. Hos. i. 4). During the reign of Ahab the conflict between the old order and the new reached its bitterest stage. The marriage of Ahab to Jezebel which sealed the alliance between Israel and Tyre brought with it a twofold challenge. On the one hand Jezebel established in the northern capital her own native Tyrian Baal cult and before long apparently attempted to constitute it as the official religion of Israel.

[1] Cf. J. Bright, op. cit., p. 211.

3

PROPHETS

The prophets who represented it enjoyed official status (1 Kings xviii. 19) and the court and ruling classes evidently supported Jezebel's innovations (1 Kings xxi. 8f.). On the national level there seems to have been widespread apostasy (1 Kings xix. 10) and the majority of the people now became strongly attached to pagan cults (1 Kings xviii. 21). Persecution of those loyal to Yahwism ensued and the prophetic party, the back-bone of resistance, became the special object of Jezebel's wrath (1 Kings xviii. 4). It is quite probable that under the pressure of the persecution many prophets hitherto faithful to the covenant faith yielded and henceforth were willing to compromise with paganism. From this time forward the danger of false prophets must have greatly increased (cf. 1 Kings xxii; Hos. ix. 8; Amos vii. 14; Mic. iii. 5–6; Isa. ix. 14, EVV 15; Zeph. iii. 4) and it is possible that the laws in Deuteronomy dealing with the problem of false prophets (Deut. xviii. 20–22) had their origin at this time.

Besides this challenge on the cultic level there was also at this time an alarming growth in social injustice. Jezebel had evidently no difficulty in having the unfortunate Naboth removed (1 Kings xxi. 7f.). And there must have been many more incidents of this nature. There is evidence of the exploitation of the poor by the richer elements in the community: the former were compelled in hard times to borrow from the latter on outrageous terms which forced them to pledge their land and even their own persons as security (2 Kings iv. 1). The whole structure of Israelite society was threatened by this harsh system. It has been plausibly suggested that the practices denounced a century later by Amos (Amos ii. 6–8; iii. 10; iv. 1; v. 11) had their beginnings at this time.[1] Under the house of Omri there were many in Israel for whom covenant law mattered little or not at all.

It was in this situation that Elijah and Elisha together with the prophetic guilds declared war on the Omrides and became instrumental in bringing about their violent downfall. Elijah on Mount Carmel championed the cause of Yahwism against the worship of the Tyrian Baal (1 Kings xviii. 17–40) and took up the sword against its cult personnel. He it was who faced Ahab and Jezebel and roundly cursed them for their treachery with Naboth (1 Kings xxi. 17–24) and it is possible that he may even have conspired with Hazael of Damascus to overthrow the house of Omri (1 Kings xix. 15–17). Elijah's struggle was carried forward by his disciple Elisha in whose days his master's dreadful curse upon Ahab and Jezebel was violently realized (2 Kings ix. 30–x. 11).

[1] Cf. J. Bright, op. cit., p. 225.

Attention has already been drawn to the prominent role occupied by the ideology of the Holy War in Deuteronomy. The grand period of this old sacral institution was the time of the Judges and it has been observed how strongly the principle of charismatic leadership so characteristic of this institution asserted itself in the course of the history of the northern kingdom. What is surely of great significance is that the ideology of the Holy War was also preserved by the prophetic party of which we have been speaking.

Saul, as we have noted, incurred Samuel's wrath and rejection for failing to carry out the sacred ban on the Amalekites (1 Sam. xiii. 13–14). Almost two centuries later Ahab is charged for similarly failing to destroy Ben Hadad (1 Kings xx. 35–43) and again in this case the rebuke came from one of the 'sons of the prophets' of whom we hear so much at this time. These guilds of prophets first make their appearance in Samuel's time; what their history before that period was we cannot tell.[1] It is not without significance, however, that they make their appearance at the height of the Philistine threat. They seem in fact to have been most active in times of military crises when the life of the nation was in peril and Yahweh's Holy War had to be waged. They appear often on the battle-field beside the armies of Israel advising the king and demanding that the wars be carried out according to the sacral principles of the Holy War (cf. 1 Kings xx. 13–14, 22, 28, 35f.; 2 Kings iii. 11f.; xiii. 14f.). It is not surprising therefore to find Elijah and Elisha referred to as 'the chariots of Israel and its horsemen' (2 Kings ii. 12; xiii. 14).

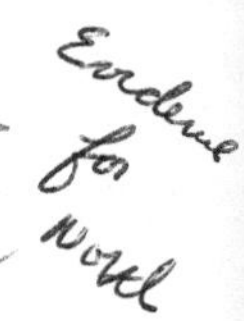

Here then we have what must be considered as vital contacts between Deuteronomy and the teaching of the prophetic party in northern Israel. They both stand upon the traditions of the old Israelite amphictyony—their concern for the observance of covenant law, their adherence to the ideology of the Holy War, their strong attachment to the principles of charismatic leadership and their critical attitude towards the monarchy. The attitude of Deuteronomy towards the institution of kingship indeed has been taken by many as one of the strongest links between it and the traditions of northern Israel.[2] The law in Deuteronomy xvii. 14f. reflects the antagonistic attitude of the northern prophetic party. Here the sacral ideas which grew up around the figure of the king in Jerusalem are entirely absent.

[1] Cf. J. Lindblom, *Prophecy in Ancient Israel* (Oxford, 1962), pp. 65ff.

[2] Cf. A. Alt, 'Die Heimat des Deuteronomiums', *Kleine Schriften*, II, pp. 266f.; G. E. Wright, *Deuteronomy*, *IB*, II, pp. 325, 441.

Further evidence of the northern origin of Deuteronomy may be adduced from the close connections between it and the Elohistic strata in the Pentateuch. Many similarities in phraseology between them have often been noted.[1] In addition to this, a common spirit underlies both of them. This is particularly manifest in their concern with the dangers of apostasy and idolatry in which they both reflect the life or death struggle with the Canaanite religion most vigorous in the northern kingdom.[2]

It has long been recognized that there are close affinities between Deuteronomy and the teaching of Hosea and it has often been claimed that the author of Deuteronomy was the spiritual heir of this great northern prophet.[3] Hosea, like Deuteronomy, stood upon the traditions of the Sinai covenant faith. He calls to remembrance Yahweh's saving deeds on Israel's behalf (xi. 1f.) and inveighs against an Israel that had failed to respond to the obligations which this placed upon her (iv. 1f.; v 3f.; vi. 7f.). Like his prophetic predecessors (cf. Hos. vi. 5; xii. 11, EVV 10) he waged war against the syncretism and apostasy which was so rife in his days (iv. 12f.; viii. 5f.) and the widespread disregard for the covenant demands. His attitude towards monarchy (cf. viii. 4) also reflects the negative point of view of Deuteronomy. But it is perhaps in the fundamental election theology of both books that they stand closest together.[4] For both of them Israel's election is simply and solely the result of Yahweh's love for her and not because she merited it in any way (Deut. vii. 7–8; Hos. xi. 1f.). This election love demanded a response from Israel in terms of love and obedience; Israel was to love Yahweh because he first loved her. Thus it is that right at the beginning of Deuteronomy is the commandment which sums up all the demands which follow in the body of the book: 'You shall love the Lord your God with all your heart, and with all your soul, and with all your might' (Deut. vi. 5). And it was because Israel had not loved Yahweh but had been unfaithful to him as an adulterous wife that Hosea saw that she was doomed.[5]

The connections between Deuteronomy and northern Israel are

[1] Cf. G. E. Wright, op. cit., p. 318.

[2] The close connections between some of the laws in Deuteronomy and E's Book of the Covenant have led to the suggestion that Deuteronomy was intended to replace it. Cf. O. Eissfeldt, *The Old Testament: An Introduction* (1965), pp. 220f.

[3] Cf. S. R. Driver, *Deuteronomy*[3] (1902), p. xxvii; A. Alt, 'Die Heimat des Deuteronomiums', *Kleine Schriften*, II, pp. 271f.

[4] Cf. A. Alt, ibid., pp. 272f.

[5] H. W. Wolff, *Hosea* (*BKAT*, Neukirchen, 1961), *passim* draws many parallels between the terminology of Hosea and Deuteronomy.

further evidenced by a consideration of its peculiar name-theology to which attention has already been drawn. In Deuteronomy the nature of Yahweh's dwelling among his people is defined in what has been called a theologically sublimated manner.[1] Not Yahweh himself but his name dwells in the sanctuary. Yahweh shall choose out a place 'to make his name to dwell there' (Deut. xii. 5, 11 *et passim*). The Deuteronomistic passage which perhaps best illustrates this is 1 Kings viii. 27f.;

> 'But will God indeed dwell on the earth? Behold, heaven and the highest heaven cannot contain thee; how much less this house which I have built! Yet have regard to the prayer of thy servant and to his supplication, O Lord my God, hearkening to the cry and to the prayer which thy servant prays before thee this day; that thy eyes may be open night and day toward this house, the place of which thou hast said "My name shall be there", that thou mayest hearken to the prayer which thy servant offers toward this place. And hearken thou to the supplication of thy people Israel, when they pray toward this place; yea, hear thou in heaven thy dwelling place; and when thou hearest, forgive.'

The idea that Yahweh's name dwells on earth is theologically in advance of the older notion that Yahweh himself would dwell in the sanctuary, a notion which seems to have had its origin in connection with the sacred Ark as the throne of the invisibly present God and which was accepted and preserved in Jerusalem after the Ark had been moved there by David (cf. Num. x. 35f.; 1 Sam. iv. 4f.; 2 Kings xix. 14f.).[2] This peculiar name-theology must therefore be seen as the theological background to the radically 'demythologized' view of the Ark in Deuteronomy x. 1f. and xxxi. 24f. where it is no longer conceived of as the throne of Yahweh, he who is 'enthroned above the Cherubim' (cf. 2 Kings xix. 15) but is merely the receptacle for the tables of the law.[3] These two passages in fact are probably the later insertion of the Deuteronomistic historian who has attempted to give the Ark, so important in the Jerusalem theology by which he was influenced, some place within the law of Moses. That in so doing he has subjected it to the name-theology is further evidence that he belongs ultimately to the same tradition as the authors of Deuteronomy

[1] Cf. G. von Rad, *Studies in Deuteronomy*, p. 39.

[2] Cf. R. E. Clements, *God and Temple* (Oxford, 1965), pp. 40f.

[3] Cf. G. von Rad, *Studies in Deuteronomy*, p. 40; R. E. Clements, *God and Temple*, pp. 88f. That the Ark was the container of the tables of the law was not in itself a new idea; it had probably always been regarded as such. But the assertion that it was only this represents a departure from the older idea that it was also the pedestal for the invisibly present Yahweh. Cf. R. E. Clements, *God and Temple*, p. 96.

however much he has been influenced by purely Jerusalem cultic traditions.[1] It is surely of great significance that the original book of Deuteronomy nowhere mentions the Ark. It is surprising, to say the least, that a book which is so steeped in the old amphictyonic traditions affords no place to the cultic object which was of such manifest importance in the life of the tribal league. What is the background to this name-theology with its consequences for the Deuteronomistic concept of the function of the Ark?

The most reasonable solution to the problem of the origin of this name-theology lies in the cultic situation brought about in northern Israel by the disruption. When David captured the Jebusite stronghold of Jerusalem and established it as his capital he took steps to bring there the sacred Ark, no doubt in order to give his city a necessary theological significance for the twelve tribes.[2] By his actions Jerusalem became the successor to the amphictyonic central shrine and heir to the sacral traditions of Israel. When, however, the schism between the north and the south took place Jeroboam I realized immediately the danger of allowing Jerusalem to maintain its spiritual supremacy. He therefore established the two rival sanctuaries of Bethel and Dan and set up the 'golden calves'. Now it is being increasingly recognized that in so doing he was innovating no new cult. The cultic emblems of the calves are now seen to have been intended to replace the Ark as the throne or pedestal of Yahweh.[3] It is possible indeed that the calf had been at a much earlier period a cultic object of some of the tribes who came to make up Israel.[4] But if Jeroboam's cultic policy was successful for a time it is clear that soon the golden calves became the object of abuse occasioned no doubt by their resemblance to the bull fertility cults of the Canaanites. The prophetic party ultimately condemned them (cf. Hos. viii. 5, 6; x 5; xiii. 2). The initial problem therefore arose once again: how can Yahweh be present among his people without the Ark? Does it not now seem very probable that it was this cultic problem in northern Israel which gave rise to the development of Deuteronomy's name theology?[5] The absence of the Ark and the

[1] For this see further below pp. 111ff.

[2] Cf. M. Noth, *The History of Israel*², p. 191; J. Bright, *A History of Israel*, pp. 179f.

[3] Cf. K. T. Obbink, 'Jahwebilder', *ZAW* 47 (1929), pp. 264–274; W. F. Albright, *From the Stone Age to Christianity*² (1946), pp. 229f.

[4] Cf. O. Eissfeldt, 'Lade und Stierbild', *ZAW* 58 (1940–41), pp. 190–215; R. de Vaux, *Ancient Israel*, pp. 333f.

[5] Cf. F. Dumermuth, 'Zur deuteronomischen Kulttheologie und ihre Voraussetzungen', *ZAW* 70 (1958), pp. 70ff.

failure of Jeroboam's golden calves were eventually replaced by the more exalted notion of Yahweh's name as the manifestation of his presence in the sanctuary. And this in turn led to a corresponding devaluation of the significance of the Ark in the Deuteronomic circles. If this is accepted then here again we have strong evidence of the northern origin of the Deuteronomic traditions.[1]

On the basis of our discussion so far it may be concluded that the book of Deuteronomy stems ultimately from northern Israel. This is clear from its affinities with both the Elohist and Hosea but above all from its strong association with the old amphictyonic traditions preserved and transmitted down through the centuries by the prophetic party in the northern kingdom. This further suggests that we must trace Deuteronomy and the Deuteronomic tradition to these prophetic circles. Such a view of the authorship of the book, however, runs contrary to the dominant trend of recent research which traces its origin to circles of levites.[2]

The most notable recent statement of the view that it is to levites in northern Israel that Deuteronomy owes its origin has come from H. W. Wolff in his short study of the background of Hosea's preaching.[3] Wolff acknowledges that Hosea stands firmly within the traditions of the prophetic party in northern Israel and that he took his place alongside the prophets in opposition to the idolatry prevalent in his days.[4] He must therefore be seen as heir of the traditions of the prophetic party. But there are certain aspects of his teaching which, according to Wolff, he could not have inherited from his prophetic predecessors, viz. his marked concern with the true and ideal function of cultic worship and his remarkable familiarity with the old sacral traditions of early Israel.[5] The prophetic circles, argues Wolff, cannot seriously be considered as the bearers of such cultic and sacral traditions.[6]

[1] It has to be acknowledged, however, that Deuteronomy's strong attachment to the ideology of the Holy War would seem to imply that the Ark, so central in this ideology, must have retained some of its older mystique for the Deuteronomic circle. This seems clear from such passages as Deut. vii. 12 where Yahweh is conceived of as being in the 'midst' of Israel in battle. Nevertheless, it is evident that in actual cultic practice the authors of Deuteronomy have dispensed with the older notion. Cf. F. Dumermuth, op. cit., p. 71 n. 66.

[2] Cf. especially, G. von Rad, *Studies in Deuteronomy*, pp. 60ff.; G. E. Wright, *Deuteronomy*, *IB*, II, pp. 325f.; H. W. Wolff, 'Hoseas geistige Heimat', *Gesammelte Studien* (Munich, 1964), pp. 232–250.

[3] H. W. Wolff, 'Hoseas geistige Heimat', *Gesammelte Studien* (Munich, 1964), pp. 232–250. See further his ' "Wissen um Gott" bei Hosea als Urform von Theologie', *Gesammelte Studien*, pp. 182–205.

[4] H. W. Wolff, 'Hoseas geistige Heimat', *Gesammelte Studien*, pp. 233f.

[5] Ibid., p. 244.

[6] Ibid., p. 244.

How then are we to account for Hosea's knowledge of these traditions? Wolff believes that he can only have gained his knowledge of them through contact with a circle of levites who had faithfully preserved them down through the years and who were, like Hosea and the prophets, in active opposition to the popular and corrupt practices of their days.[1] Such a circle may have originated among the levites who, according to 1 Kings xii. 31f., were expelled by Jeroboam I from Bethel and Dan.[2] It is further suggested that Shechem may have been the centre of this levitical group.[3]

Wolff maintains that it was from these levites that Hosea acquired his knowledge of Israel's sacral traditions and his high concept of the proper function of cult in the life of the people.[4] His condemnation of the official priesthood of his time is based upon his conviction that it was failing to fulfil the function demanded of it by Yahweh to teach Israel the 'knowledge of God' which, according to Wolff, consisted of the knowledge or actualization of the *magnalia dei*, the history of the saving deeds in exodus and conquest, together with the covenant laws.[5] Finally, it is suggested that the teaching of this levitical circle eventually found expression in the book of Deuteronomy.[6]

But the evidence upon which this view is based must be considered very tenuous. There is, to begin with, no mention, not even the slightest hint, of such a group of faithful levites in Hosea's recorded oracles; only the activity of the prophets is mentioned (cf. Hos. vi. 4–6; ix. 7–9; xii. 11, EVV 10). It is surely inconceivable that the prophet would have failed to leave some record of a circle of priests from whom, on Wolff's hypothesis, he derived so much of his teaching. And by the same token, if Shechem was the centre of such a group and the place where the covenant faith was kept alive and actualized during those dark days, then it is astonishing that there is no mention of this in Hosea (nor indeed in the rest of the Old Testament!) but only the rather vague reference in Hosea vi. 9 which may indeed suggest, as we have seen, that the priesthood at this sanctuary was guilty of the most heinous crimes.[7] As to the conjectured origin of such a group, can we seriously accord historicity

[1] H. W. Wolff, op. cit., pp. 244f.
[2] Ibid., pp. 244–245.
[3] Ibid., p. 249 n. 70.
[4] Ibid., pp. 245f.
[5] Cf. H. W. Wolff, ' "Wissen um Gott" bei Hosea als Urform von Theologie' *Gesammelte Studien*, pp. 182–205 and 'Hoseas geistige Heimat', ibid., p. 246. See above p. 64 n. 1.
[6] H. W. Wolff, 'Hoseas geistige Heimat', *Gesammelte Studien*, pp. 248–250.
[7] Cf. N. W. Porteous, 'Actualization and the Prophetic Criticism of the Cult', *Tradition und Situation* (ed. E. Würthwein and O. Kaiser, 1963), p. 100.

to the narrative in 1 Kings xii. 31ff. of Jeroboam's expulsion of the levites from Bethel and the institution of priests 'from among all the people' in their place? The passage is clearly highly Deuteronomistic and for the Deuteronomist Jeroboam was the arch-villain in the history of Israel and the source of those sins which led ultimately to the destruction and exile of the nation (cf. 2 Kings xvii. 22f.). Nothing that this king did can be commended as far as the Deuteronomist is concerned. The charge that he instituted non-levitic priests in Bethel is, however, very improbable for several reasons. It seems quite clear that Jeroboam's cultic policy in establishing Bethel and Dan as state sanctuaries was to weaken the attraction of Jerusalem, now the location of the sacred Ark, for his subjects lest its religious primacy should perpetuate its political centrality and lead to trouble in his own newly established kingdom (1 Kings xii. 26f.). But it is equally clear that Bethel and Dan were constituted as official *Yahweh* sanctuaries to challenge the supremacy of the southern capital and that Jeroboam did not, as the Deuteronomistic historian would have us believe (1 Kings xii. 28f.), attempt to set up pagan cults in these places. To have done so would surely have led to his own immediate undoing! And on the same grounds, it is clearly improbable that he would have expelled the levites and have instituted his own arbitrary priesthood in their stead (what possible motive could he have had for doing so?). To have made such an innovation would have been an act of the greatest foolishness—and consequences. That the priesthood at Bethel was legitimate seems also quite clear from the fact that in the century after Jeroboam, Elijah and Elisha and the prophetic guilds were closely associated with this sanctuary. Nowhere in the sagas of these prophets is there any indication that they regarded or condemned the priests at Bethel as impostors. The same is true also of both Amos and Hosea who charge the priesthood at this place of many things but never of being non-levitic.[1]

Finally, Wolff's suggestion that Hosea could have acquired his knowledge of Israel's sacral and cultic traditions only from levites must be questioned in the light of what we have attempted to show in the preceding pages of this chapter, viz. the close connection between the prophets in the period before Hosea and the cult. Beginning with Samuel and continuing down through the period of Elijah, Elisha and the prophetic guilds there is considerable evidence to show that the prophetic party carried out its functions to some extent at least at cult centres such as Bethel, Gilgal and Mizpah.

[1] Cf. F. Dumermuth, op. cit., pp. 81ff.

In view of this it is surely reasonable to suppose that the prophetic party itself would have been in full possession of a knowledge of the old traditions and that Hosea and his contemporaries in the prophetic office would have inherited this knowledge from their predecessors. If this is accepted then there is clearly no necessity to conjecture that Hosea derived such knowledge from levitical circles.

The most reasonable solution to the problem of the connections between Hosea and Deuteronomy is best understood if we see both as deriving ultimately from the same source—the teaching of the prophetic party in northern Israel. This is further substantiated by another consideration. For Hosea Moses was the first of the prophets:

> 'By a prophet the Lord brought Israel up from Egypt,
> And by a prophet he was preserved.'
>
> (Hos. xii. 14, EVV 13)

Now it is significant that in Deuteronomy also Moses is the prophet *par excellence:*

> 'I will raise up for them a prophet like you from among their brethren; and I will put my words in his mouth, and he shall speak to them all that I command him.'
>
> (Deut. xviii. 18)

Indeed it is precisely here that the prophetic origin of Deuteronomy is most strongly in evidence. Attention has already been drawn to the remarkable influence which the covenant festival has exercised upon the form of Deuteronomy. Now it is widely accepted that one of the most important cultic functionaries in this festival was the covenant mediator through whom and by whom Yahweh's will and demands were made known to the cult assembly.[1] It has been plausibly suggested that Exodus xx. 18–21 may contain the aetiology for this office:[2]

> 'Now when all the people perceived the thunderings and the lightnings and the sound of the trumpet and the mountain smoking, the people were afraid and trembled; and they stood afar off and said to Moses, "You speak to us, and we will hear; but let not God speak to us, lest we die." And Moses said to the people, "Do not fear; for God has come to prove you, and that the fear of him may be before your eyes, that you

[1] Cf. H.-J. Kraus, *Worship in Israel* (Oxford, 1966), pp. 106ff; M. Newman, 'The Prophetic Call of Samuel' in *Israel's Prophetic Heritage* (ed. B. W. Anderson and W. H. Harrelson, London, 1962), pp. 86ff.

[2] Cf. H.-J. Kraus, op. cit., pp. 108f.; M. Newman, op. cit., pp. 87f.

may not sin." And the people stood afar off, while Moses drew near to the thick darkness where God was.'

On the basis of this it may be adduced that in the festival the covenant mediator performed the following role:

1. To speak for and in the name of Yahweh to the people (Exod. xx. 1–2a.)
2. To recite the *Heilsgeschichte* (Exod. xx. 2, xix. 3–6).
3. To proclaim the divine laws binding upon the covenant community (Exod. xx. 3ff.).

It seems clear that this was the function which Joshua performed at Shechem (Joshua xxiv). The people presented themselves 'before God' (Joshua xxiv. 1). In verses 2–13 Joshua recites the *Heilsgeschichte*, in verses 14–15, 23, he exhorts the assembly to be faithful to Yahweh alone and in 16–18, 21 the people respond to this appeal. Finally, in verse 25 Joshua is said to have 'made a covenant with the people that day, and made statutes and ordinances for them at Shechem'.

Now the significant factor from our point of view is that Deuteronomy itself provides for this office and assigns it to the prophet and not to the priest:

> 'The Lord your God will raise up for you a prophet like me from among you, from your brethren—him you shall heed—just as you desired of the Lord your God at Horeb on the day of assembly, when you said, "Let me not hear again the voice of the Lord my God, or see this great fire any more, lest I die." And the Lord said to me, "They have rightly said all that they have spoken. I will raise up for them a prophet like you from among their brethren; and I will put my words in his mouth, and he shall speak to them all that I command him."'
>
> (Deut. xviii. 15–18; cf. v. 4f.)

In other words, the function exercised by Moses in Deuteronomy is that of prophetic covenant mediator. What is more, this office is conceived of in Deuteronomy as being permanently established; Yahweh will 'raise up' prophets to succeed Moses as covenant mediator. That is to say, Deuteronomy here pre-figures Moses as the first of a succession of prophets who exercised this office in Israel.

What is the origin of this concept of the prophetic covenant mediator? The period of the tribal league offers no direct light. At this time it is possible that the minor judges (Judges x. 1–5; xii. 7–15) performed this function. Such texts as Deuteronomy xxvii. 9f., 14f., xxxi. 9–13 may be an indication that levites at one time were the covenant mediators. But there is reason to believe that beginning with Samuel the office was assumed by the prophets.[1] The narrative of Samuel's call in 1 Samuel iii. 1–iv. 1a may indeed contain the aetiology of this. The central purpose of the narrative is to relate how the house of Eli was rejected by Yahweh and the young Samuel chosen to be its successor—'And all Israel from Dan to Beersheba knew that Samuel was established as a prophet of the Lord. And the Lord appeared again at Shiloh, for the Lord revealed himself to Samuel at Shiloh by the word of the Lord' (1 Sam. iii. 20f.). Thus Samuel would have taken upon himself the function of covenant mediator which we may presume to have been previously exercised by Eli and his predecessors.

That Samuel carried out these functions seems clear from several passages in the Old Testament. It has already been observed that after the collapse of the tribal league he 'judged Israel' at several cult centres and that this same expression is employed to designate the office of the minor judges at an earlier time. Samuel must therefore be seen as successor to these older cultic functionaries. This is further substantiated by a consideration of the narrative of the assembly at Gilgal over which he presided (1 Sam. xi. 14–xii. 25).[2] The issue at stake was the demand for the establishment of a monarchy in Israel. As in Joshua xxiv., 'all Israel' is assembled 'before Yahweh'. In xii. 1–5 Samuel reminds the people of this faithfulness to the covenant demands. In verses 6–13 he recites the *Heilsgeschichte* concluding with a reference to the Ammonite threat and its upshot in the demand for a king and the granting of this request. The new order is established and there follows the covenantal order of the kingdom together with Samuel's exhortation to the people and king to be faithful to Yahweh together with the promise of blessing for such a faithfulness and the warning of punishment for disobedience (*vv.* 14f.). In verses 16–18 Samuel invokes Yahweh to send thunder and rain as a sign of his displeasure with the people's demand for a king. The people then ask Samuel to intercede for them and he, as covenant mediator, accedes to their request once more exhorting them to faithfulness (*vv.* 19–25).

Here then is some evidence of Samuel's role as covenant mediator. At Gilgal he performed the same functions as Moses did at Sinai (Exod. xixf.) and on the plains of Moab (Deuteronomy) and Joshua at Shechem (Joshua xxiv). Samuel is therefore conceived of here as

[1] For much of what follows see M. Newman, op. cit., pp. 86ff.

[2] For this see J. Muilenburg, 'The form and structure of the covenantal formulations', *VT* 9 (1959), pp. 347–365.

a second Moses, just as Joshua is represented also as Moses's successor.[1]

There is some evidence too that at a still later time yet another prophet performs the role of covenant mediator. Elijah's contest with the prophets of Baal on Mount Carmel is certainly reminiscent of the covenant assembly as depicted in Joshua xxiv and 1 Samuel xii.[2] As at Shechem and Gilgal, 'all the people of Israel' have gathered at Carmel (1 Kings xviii. 19). Here too Elijah, like Joshua and Samuel, exhorts Israel to obedience to the covenant God (xviii. 21). And as at Shechem so here the people respond to the prophet's appeal by acclaiming Yahweh as their God (xviii. 39). It is significant that Elijah built a stone altar upon which sacrifice is offered as Joshua had done at Shechem.

Accordingly it may be concluded that there is considerable evidence in support of the view that the function of covenant mediator was exercised by the prophets. And is this not of great significance in the discussion of the authorship of Deuteronomy? We have seen that it was primarily the prophetic party in the northern kingdom which kept alive the old amphictyonic traditions which underlie the book. The evidence for this is abundant. When we add to this the fact that the very role exercised by Moses in Deuteronomy is that of prophet then it is surely difficult to escape the conclusion that the book originated in prophetic rather than priestly circles. In Deuteronomy Moses is the prophet *par excellence.*

Here then we have what must be considered to be a good case for the theory that the book of Deuteronomy owes its origin to prophetic circles in northern Israel. But it leaves several important issues unanswered. It will be clear that such a view of the provenance and authorship of the book accounts for many of its basic characteristics but by no means all. In particular, the demand for the centralization of the cult was never, as far as we know, a principle of these prophetic circles. How then are we to explain its presence in Deuteronomy? And one further crucial question remains to be answered: if, as this view suggests, Deuteronomy derived from northern circles, then how did it come to be in the Jerusalem Temple in 621 B.C. and how, furthermore, did it there become the basis of a reformation carried out by the Judaean monarch and supported by the Jerusalem priesthood? These are questions which demand an answer if the problem of Deuteronomy is to be satisfactorily dealt with. What they

[1] Cf. J. Muilenburg, ibid., p. 364.
[2] Cf. M. Newman, op. cit., pp. 94ff.

amount to is basically this: has Deuteronomy after all any connections with Judah from a theological point of view? Is it possible that although the book has strong affinities with north Israelite traditions it may also have been influenced by specifically Judaean traditions?

The answer given to this question by A. Alt is a firm No.[1] Alt argues that the book of Deuteronomy was the reformation programme of a revival movement in northern Israel following the fall of Samaria in 721 B.C.[2] According to this view the representatives of this revival movement may have had the whole of the erstwhile kingdom of Israel in mind or just that part of it which was still occupied by Israelites, or perhaps one individual province. If this last suggestion is correct then the province may have been Samaria. Alt suggests that this would account for Deuteronomy's marked interest in Shechem which may therefore have been the sanctuary in the mind of those who formulated the centralization law.[3]

Several considerations, however, render this theory unacceptable. Alt draws attention to the narrow estimation of the institution of monarchy in Deuteronomy and rightly sees in it the same attitude which we have seen to be typical of the northern prophetical circles.[4] As he views it, the author of Deuteronomy whilst himself disapproving of the monarchy was nevertheless forced to tolerate it and to attempt somehow to give it a place in the reformation programme though quite clearly he does so with severe reservations. But it is just here that Alt raises a serious difficulty in his own thesis. If, as he argues, Deuteronomy is the product of a revival movement in northern Israel some time after 721 B.C. then what possible need could there have been for the authors of such a movement to consider monarchy at all? With the destruction of the state had come the end of monarchy. Why then did not the authors of Deuteronomy, if they were preparing for a revival in northern Israel, simply condemn outright kingship as one of those factors which had led to the recent catastrophe and, in keeping with the nature of Deuteronomy as the address of Moses, formulate a law which prohibits the establishment of monarchy in Israel? One cannot avoid the feeling that when the author of Deuteronomy drew up the law concerning monarchy (Deut. xvii. 14f.) he was dealing with an existing institution which, whatever his own wishes, had to be reckoned with as

[1] A. Alt, 'Die Heimat des Deuteronomiums', *Kleine Schriften*, II (1953), pp. 250–275.
[2] Ibid., pp. 273f.
[3] Ibid., p. 274 and footnote on the same page.
[4] Ibid., pp. 263–268. See further his 'Das Königtum in den Reichen Israel und Juda', *Kleine Schriften*, II, pp. 116–134.

part of the life of the people among whom he lived and for whom, presumably, he was legislating.

Another weakness in Alt's theory is his failure to deal with the question of how this alleged northern revival programme came to be in Jerusalem in the reign of Josiah. Here again he raises a difficulty for his own thesis. Alt is at pains to emphasize that it is incorrect to imagine that the Assyrian deportation had so decimated or weakened the northern population that it was incapable of any further religious movements.[1] Now the obvious question is: if, as Alt argues, Deuteronomy was drawn up as a reformation programme in and exclusively for the north then why was it not adopted and put into operation by the strongly Israelite population which he believes to have been untouched by the Assyrian deportation? This makes all the more necessary some attempt to explain how Deuteronomy came to be in the southern kingdom in 621 B.C. But it has to be asked if Alt is not being rather over optimistic about the strength of the Israelite population left in the northern kingdom after 721 B.C. The record in 2 Kings xvii. 24ff. concerning the necessity laid upon the Assyrian authorities to send back an Israelite priest to minister to the foreigners settled around Bethel who did not know 'the law of the god of the land' would seem to indicate a severe lack of religious leadership in the country. In addition, the fact that as far as our sources are concerned any revival movements amongst Israelites during the century or more between the fall of Samaria and the destruction of Jerusalem in 586 B.C. came from Judah and not the north surely indicates that the real strength of the nation and its hopes for the future lay in the southern kingdom. It was Hezekiah and then Josiah who attempted to reform and revive. What is more, if we can rely on the narrative in 2 Chronicles xxx. 10, it would appear that the northerners were never very co-operative in such reformation movements stemming from Judah.

F. Dumermuth has avoided some of the difficulties into which Alt's thesis runs by arguing that Deuteronomy is the programme of a revival movement in the northern kingdom before 721 B.C.[2] According to Dumermuth Bethel was the centre of the reformation circle and the central shrine behind the centralization law.[3] But such a theory can hardly be tenable. Already in the time of both Amos and Hosea Bethel had evidently become corrupt with pagan practices

[1] A. Alt, 'Die Heimat des Deuteronomiums', op. cit., pp. 273f.
[2] F. Dumermuth, op. cit., pp. 59f.
[3] Ibid., pp. 79f.

(Hos. iv. 15; Amos iv. 4–5). It is surely inconceivable that if Bethel was the centre of a revival and reformation movement in the period before 721 B.C. Hosea could have referred to it as Bethaven! And this theory also leaves unanswered the question of how the Deuteronomic traditions moved south and were there put into effect.

We are left therefore with our initial problem, viz. if, as we have reason to believe, Deuteronomy had its origins among the prophetic party of the northern kingdom, how did it find its way to Judah? Is it possible that the book has after all been influenced to some extent at least by specifically Judaean traditions, especially those centring on Mount Zion? It is to a consideration of this problem together with some recent theories suggesting a possible Judaean provenance of Deuteronomy that we must now turn.

CHAPTER V

DEUTERONOMY AND JUDAH

THE traditio-historical investigation of Deuteronomy has revealed that the book has as its basis the sacral and cultic traditions of the old Israelite amphictyony and that it probably owes its origin to prophetic circles in northern Israel by whom these traditions were preserved and transmitted during the period of the monarchy. At the same time it is clear that such a theory of the provenance and authorship of the book leaves certain vital issues unanswered. In particular it raises the question of how it came to be in Jerusalem in the late seventh century and of how it was there accepted by the Judaean authorities as the will of Yahweh for his people. It has also become clear that although such a view satisfies the basic nature of Deuteronomy as the deposit of the amphictyonic traditions, it does not account for other aspects of the book, especially the demand for the centralization of the cult which, as far as we know, was never advocated by any northern circle whether priestly or prophetic. No theory of the origin of Deuteronomy is complete without a consideration of these problems.

The fundamental question involved is this: is it possible that Deuteronomy had after all some associations with Judaean circles or was at least influenced by Judaean traditions? Or, to go further, is it possible that in view of the role played by the book in the Josianic reformation its origins must be sought among specifically Judaean circles?

Two recent studies, by G. von Rad and O. Bächli,[1] have advanced the theory that Deuteronomy originated amongst Judaean circles and we may begin our consideration of this problem with a discussion of their views.

Von Rad has proposed a theory which in contrast to the predominant view of recent years finds the provenance of Deuteronomy among circles of levites in the Judaean countryside in the seventh century B.C.[2] On the basis of a form-critical analysis of the book von

[1] G. von Rad, *Studies in Deuteronomy* (London, 1953); O. Bächli, *Israel und die Völker: eine Studie zum Deuteronomium* (Zürich, 1962).

[2] G. von Rad, *Studies in Deuteronomy*, pp. 60ff.

Rad concludes that it has a two-fold nature. On the one hand it contains a great deal of old cultic material, series of apodeictic commandments and priestly *toroth*, all of which has been worked over and presented homiletically.[1] In addition to this he sees Deuteronomy as being impregnated with the ideology of the old sacral institution of the Holy War which has imparted to the book a decidedly martial nature.[2] The many laws and speeches dealing with this old institution and the cultic form in which the book is cast—its basic pattern follows the old covenant festival—as well as other old cultic norms point, in von Rad's opinion, to the old Yahweh amphictyony for their origin.[3] Accordingly it is concluded that the authors of Deuteronomy were the bearers of a priestly and cultic tradition, stemming ultimately from the period of the tribal league, together with a national and martial spirit. Von Rad believes that any answer to the question of the origin of the book must satisfy this peculiar double form, this 'Janus-like' quality.

For von Rad the custodians of such a priestly and cultic tradition can only have been levites. Only priests, it is maintained, could have had access to such a wide range of cultic material and, more important still, only priests could have had the authority to expound and re-interpret these old traditions and laws in the free manner in which the authors of Deuteronomy have treated them.[4] The striking homiletic style in which the book is written points for its origin to a preaching activity and this was carried out, he argues, by a body of levites living in the country areas of Judah who were the bearers of the old patriarchal traditions underlying Deuteronomy and who were at the same time the representatives of a revival movement in Judah in the seventh century B.C.[5] That the levites engaged in such preaching activity is evidenced by such texts as Nehemiah viii. 7f. and 2 Chronicles xxxv. 3 which, though post-exilic, no doubt reflect, it is argued, much earlier practice going back to the pre-exilic period.[6]

If these arguments concerning the activity of levites satisfy the cultic aspects of Deuteronomy, what about the other aspect, the martial and nationalistic nature of the book? Von Rad attempts to account for this by claiming that these levites were the spokesmen of a movement for national revival and independence amongst the 'people of the land' who, according to E. Würthwein,[7] were the

[1] G. von Rad, op. cit., chapter I. [2] Ibid., chapter IV. [3] Ibid., p. 40.
[4] Ibid., p. 24. [5] Ibid., pp. 66f.
[6] Ibid., pp. 13f. Cf. his *Old Testament Theology*, I (London, 1962), pp. 72f.
[7] E. Würthwein, *Der 'am ha 'arez im Alten Testament*, *BWANT* IV:17 (Stuttgart, 1936).

body of free, property-owning, full (male) citizens of Judah.[1] Following E. Junge,[2] von Rad believes that this body came to power in 701 B.C. when Sennacherib's destruction of Judah's regular mercenary army necessitated the revival of the old militia which was drawn from the ranks of these landed gentry.[3] He argues that this body aimed at national independence and at the same time inner religious renewal: 'the old patriarchal traditions of the strict Yahweh faith had long remained alive amongst the free peasant population, and had given rise to an opposition to the capital which expressed itself in strong impulses towards revival in both cult and politics'.[4] This movement must not therefore be viewed as having its centre in Jerusalem, a fact which is further evidenced by the very insignificant role accorded the king in Deuteronomy—a role which clearly cannot reflect the sacral concepts of kingship which were characteristic of the Jerusalem traditions and ideology surrounding the Davidic monarchy.[5]

Von Rad thus arrives at the conclusion that the authors of Deuteronomy are to be sought among the levites living in the Judaean countryside in the seventh century who were the bearers of the old sacral and cultic traditions underlying the book and who represented a strong movement for national revival and independence among the 'people of the land'. This movement for reform and revival in both cult and politics was motivated by 'a determination to reconstruct over against the desultory political experiments of the capital', that is, Jerusalem.[6]

It seems clear that von Rad believes this movement, if not itself belonging to Jerusalem, to have centred its reformation programme around the capital. It is precisely here, however, that a serious question mark may be placed against his thesis for it must be asked why country levites would have abolished their own local shrines in favour of a centralized cult and thus, as von Rad himself so aptly puts it, have sawn off the branch upon which they sat. His reply to this is twofold. In the first place it is argued that the demand for centralization in Deuteronomy rests upon a very narrow basis only and is, from the point of view of literary criticism, easy to remove as a late and final adaptation of many layers of material.[7] But the obvious objection to this is that it is precisely this late and final

[1] Cf. G. von Rad, *Studies in Deuteronomy*, pp. 66f.
[2] E. Junge, *Der Wiederaufbau des Heerwesens des Reiches Juda unter Josia*, *BWANT* IV: 23 (Stuttgart, 1937).
[3] G. von Rad, *Studies in Deuteronomy*, pp. 60f.
[4] Ibid., p. 66.
[5] Ibid., p. 62.
[6] Ibid., pp. 61–62.
[7] Ibid., p. 67.

adaptation of many layers of material which constitutes the book of Deuteronomy. If, as he maintains, the country levites were responsible for the composition of the book then they were also *a fortiori* responsible for the formulation of the centralization law in the book. His second argument is that by the time Deuteronomy made its appearance these country levites had possibly outgrown the cultic sphere proper and were now busying themselves with the scholarly preservation and transmission of the old traditions.[1] But is such a view really tenable? There is no evidence whatsoever to suggest that they were no longer ministering in the conventional manner at the local shrines. On the contrary, there is an abundance of evidence to indicate that the seventh century in Judah was a time of vigorous cultic activity. That the local sanctuaries were thriving is quite clear from the fact that Josiah had to attempt to abolish them in spite of Hezekiah's measures less than a century before. Furthermore, Deuteronomy itself makes provision for the rural priests to minister at the central shrine (Deut. xviii. 6f.). This together with the recurring commendation of their needs to the people surely implies that hitherto they had gained their livelihood at the local altars which were now to be abolished. It could be argued against this of course that not all levites in the country districts would have been involved in the reformation movement. But this would only serve to increase the difficulties in von Rad's theory for it would necessitate postulating a group of non-cultic levites who stood outside the normal functions of the priesthood in Judah. To do so would obviously be sheer conjecture without a shred of support from the records of the period with which we are concerned.

What then of von Rad's suggestion concerning the 'people of the land'? It may be said right at the outset that in the present writer's opinion far too much has been read into the meaning of this expression in the Old Testment and that those theories which regard it as a *terminus technicus* designating a fixed social or political group within the population of Judah are going beyond the evidence.[2]

[1] G. von Rad, op. cit., pp. 67–68.

[2] For various treatments of the expression as a technical term see especially the following: M. Sulzberger, *The Am Ha-aretz: the Ancient Hebrew Parliament* (Philadelphia, 1909) and 'The Polity of the Ancient Hebrews', *JQR* 3 (1912–13), pp. 1–81; N. Sloush, 'Representative Government among the Hebrews and Phoenicians', *JQR* 4 (1913) pp. 303–310; E. Klamroth, *Die jüdischen Exulanten in Babylonien*, *BWAT*, 10 (1912), pp. 99f.; E. Gillischewski, 'Der Ausdruck עם־הארץ im A. T.', *ZAW* 40 (1922), pp. 137–142; A. Menes, *Die vorexilischen Gesetze Israels im Zusammenhang seiner kulturgeschichtlichen Entwicklung*, *BZAW* 50 (1928), pp. 70f.; S. Daiches, 'The meaning of am ha-aretz in the Old Testament', *JTS* 30 (1929), pp. 245–249; R. Gordis, 'Sectional Rivalry in the Kingdom of

Quite apart from this, however, any idea that these people stand behind Deuteronomy's reformation programme must be rejected for several reasons. There is, for example, much evidence to show that the Judaean countryside was rife with all sorts of pagan cults during the seventh century B.C. One obvious indication of this is the various cults which Josiah had to get rid of (cf. 2 Kings xxiii) as well as the fact that in spite of his attempts his death was followed by a resurgence of idolatry perhaps on a worse scale than before (cf. Jer. vii. 17–18; xi. 9–13; etc. Ezek. viii). If the 'people of the land' were, as von Rad believes, a powerful political and military group seeking national independence and inner religious renewal, then surely there would have been a drastic reduction of all this paganism? On the contrary, however—and von Rad has evidently overlooked this—such texts as Jeremiah xxxiv. 19, xxxvii. 2, xliv. 21 make it abundantly clear that the 'people of the land' contributed in no small measure to the sorry state of the nation's cultic life and the depths to which it had sunk at this time!

A further weakness in this theory consists in the manner in which the Deuteronomic reformation programme was promulgated. Why, if the circles behind it formed both the political and military as well as the economic strength of the state at this time[1] was it necessary for them to deposit their programme for revival in the Jerusalem Temple in the hope that eventually it would be discovered and its demands implemented by the Jerusalem authorities? Surely, on von Rad's hypothesis, they would have required nothing more than to wait until the time was ripe—presumably when the Assyrian power in Judah was declining—and then introduce and enforce their own plans for revival and reform? If, as von Rad argues, they possessed the political and military strength in Judah then who in the capital could have resisted their intentions to reconstruct over against its alleged 'desultory political experiments'?

For these reasons, therefore, von Rad's suggestions must be considered unacceptable. Such a theory involves too many questions of a fundamental nature to be a satisfactory solution to the problem on hand. Furthermore, it quite clearly does not account for the strong associations between Deuteronomy and north Israelite traditions and literature to which attention has been drawn.

[1] Cf. G. von Rad, *Studies in Deuteronomy*, pp. 63f.

Judah', *JQR* 25 (1934–35), pp. 237–259; E. Würthwein, op. cit.; M. Pope in *IDB* (New York, 1962), I, pp. 106f. For a critique of the various views presented by these scholars see my article 'The Meaning of the Expression עם־הארץ in the Old Testament', *JSS* 10 (1965), pp. 59–66.

The dominant view of recent research into the problem of the provenance of Deuteronomy is that wherever else it came from it cannot have originated among specifically Jerusalem circles, mainly on account of the difference between the basic traditions underlying it and those centring on Mount Zion and the Davidic monarchy which had their home in Jerusalem. Recently this view has been challenged in a study of the problem by O. Bächli who has argued that Deuteronomy is the written deposit, not the cause or even partly the cause, of the Josianic reformation and the expression of specifically Jerusalem traditions.[1]

According to this theory the book of Deuteronomy originated in a period of crisis of the most dangerous potentiality. It is concerned throughout with the survival of Israel as Yahweh's people at a time when her very existence as such was threatened. This concern forms the background of the book the aim of which is to create some sort of means of meeting and averting the possible catastrophe with which the nation was evidently confronted.[2] Its authors set about their task by assembling all the powers at their command in an attempt to revive the nation in both cult and politics and to fortify it against the perils latent in the events of their day.

Bächli discerns in the book four ways in which its authors have attempted to achieve their aims, viz. by preaching which is represented in the abundance of parenetic material in the book with its recurring and urgent exhortations to faithfulness, its promises, threats and warnings;[3] in the laws governing the life and institutions of the nation;[4] in the strict cultic requirements and the laws ordering Israel's worship of Yahweh;[5] and finally in the marked political atmosphere which pervades the book with its concern for Israel's existence over against the nations, discernible in the statements demanding the destruction of the peoples amongst whom she is to settle in the promised land, and in the large amount of material dealing with the Holy War.[6] Deuteronomy is thus vitally interested in every aspect of Israel's life—both sacred and secular, political and military. The question of its authorship therefore becomes, for Bächli, one of deciding who had such an overall concern with Israel's life and who had the authority to promulgate such a comprehensive attempt to revive and reform the nation.

Bächli defines the issue by isolating the four main types of material in Deuteronomy—the parenetic, legal, cultic, and politico-military—

[1] O. Bächli, op. cit. [2] Ibid., p. 181. [3] Ibid., pp. 70–82.
[4] Ibid., pp. 82–94. [5] Ibid., pp. 94–104. [6] Ibid., pp. 104–111.

and then attempting to determine who was responsible for each of them and combined all of them.

1. *The parenesis.* Who was responsible for the preaching activity which underlies the homiletic style in which Deuteronomy is written? Bächli sees this functionary as standing between the prophet and the priest. From the latter he gained his knowledge of Israel's sacral traditions which are alluded to frequently in the parenesis, whilst from the former he inherited the office of actualizing these traditions, of making them relevant for the age in which he lived.[1] The solution to the question of who this was lies, in Bächli's opinion, in the law of the king in Deuteronomy xvii. 14–20. Here, it is argued, the king is charged with the responsibility of reading and interpreting the law in public.[2] He thus assumes the office of the law-preacher of an earlier period and as custodian and teacher of the law he is mediator between Yahweh and the people and responsible for the renewing of the covenant.[3] In this the king is clothed with the authority of Moses and is successor to the earlier 'judge of Israel'.[4]

Bächli points to the similar role played by Joshua and Samuel and, more significant for his purposes, Solomon.[5] Indeed it is precisely with the latter, he argues, that we have the last great address to 'all the assembly of Israel' before the nation was divided by the disruption (cf. 1 Kings viii. 14ff.).[6] With Solomon the series is broken until at a much later period Josiah performs the function and reads the book of the law before the people (2 Kings xxiii. 2).[7] What happened in the centuries between Solomon and Josiah is unknown. Bächli holds that all through this period the office belonged *de jure* to the monarch who probably, however, dispensed with it, perhaps because of the disruption, or delegated it to another authority, perhaps the priesthood (cf. Deut. xxxi. 9–13).[8]

2. *The law.* Bächli believes that the king was also ultimately responsible for the administration of law. He was the juridical head of the nation. Such a centralization of legal authority is witnessed to in the pre-monarchical period, it is argued, in the incident recorded in Judges xi. 4f. where Jephthah is elected head of the Gileadites, whilst at the advent of the monarchy Saul is designated as head of the tribes of Israel (1 Sam. xv. 17). Deuteronomy xvii. 8–13 (especially *vv.* 9 and 12) points to the king as judge although of course in actual practice the law would have been administered and

[1] Ibid., pp. 186f.
[2] Ibid., pp. 88f., 187f.
[3] Ibid., p. 187.
[4] Ibid., p. 187.
[5] Ibid., pp. 187f.
[6] Ibid., pp. 187–188.
[7] Ibid., pp. 188f.
[8] Ibid., p. 188.

enforced by officials who were subject to the king and exercised their functions in his name.[1]

3. *The cult.* To whom are we to look for the representatives of Deuteronomy's vital concern for the cult? Who possessed the authority to reform and regulate it in the manner demanded by Deuteronomy? Here again Bächli points to the king as the highest and ultimate authority in cultic matters in Israel. He adduces evidence for this view from the authority wielded by Ahaz (2 Kings xvi. 10f.) in not only erecting the Assyrian-type altar in the Temple but also in officiating at the sacrifices offered upon it and in regulating the cultic programme centring on it.[2] He points further to Hezekiah's attempt to abolish the local high places and Manasseh's re-erection of them (2 Kings xviii. 4, 22; xxi. 3) as well as the initiative taken by Josiah in the reformation movement in his reign.[3] Once more it is argued that the king delegated his functions in this sphere to the priesthood although at the high points in Israel's cultic calendar, especially the covenant festival, he himself would have officiated.[4]

4. *Deuteronomy's politico-military nature.* Who stands behind Deuteronomy's pronounced political and military atmosphere with its frequent statements concerning the extermination of the indigenous population of the promised land and the large amount of material centring on the ideology of the Holy War? Who was vitally concerned, as Deuteronomy is, with Israel's existence among the nations? As in the case of the parenesis, the law and the cult, Bächli once again argues that the figure behind this aspect of the book is the king.[5] This, it is contended, is clear in the case of David and even more so in the case of Josiah whose military-political activities are well in evidence. His expansion of the boundaries of his own state to include the territory of the erstwhile northern kingdom as well as his final and ill-fated conflict with Necho at Megiddo substantiate this view. The power to enforce the king's policies in this direction lay with the 'people of the land' from whose ranks the military strength of the nation was derived.[6]

Bächli thus arrives at the conclusion that the Judaean monarchy was *de jure* if not always *de facto* responsible for the various functions which the book of Deuteronomy portrays Moses as having exercised. Josiah at least made some attempt to perform them—he was teacher and preacher of the law, judge, royal priest, and the centre of

[1] Ibid., pp. 189f.
[2] Ibid., p. 193.
[3] Ibid., p. 193.
[4] Ibid., p. 194.
[5] Ibid., pp. 194f.
[6] Ibid., pp. 195, 196.

political and military power.[1] Accordingly, it is argued, the authors of Deuteronomy, for reasons which are later explained, have ascribed to Moses the functions for which the Davidic monarchy was ideally responsible.

Where then and when did Deuteronomy originate and who were its authors? Bächli's solution to this problem proceeds from the view that the book is based upon the fusion of two sets of traditions. On the one hand, it seeks to promulgate the Sinai/Mosaic covenant traditions and on the other, in prefiguring Moses as performing the ideal functions of the Judaean monarchy, it is anchored to the Davidic/Jerusalem traditions.[2] Thus the fusion in the book of Kings of these two sets of traditions to which von Rad has drawn attention[3] must already be seen, according to Bächli, in Deuteronomy itself.[4] Such a fusion clearly points for its origin to Jerusalem where, in Bächli's opinion, both traditions were united in the person of the Davidic king.[5] Accordingly, it is concluded that the book of Deuteronomy as the expression of this fusion originated among circles in Jerusalem.

As to when the book was composed, Bächli argues that whilst there is a direct relationship between the Josianic reformation and Deuteronomy we cannot regard the latter as the basis of the former. On the contrary, Deuteronomy was composed after the reformation and was the deposit of it.[6] According to this view the tragic death of Josiah at Megiddo and the reaction against the reformation which subsequently set in moved those who had been involved in Josiah's cultic and political aims to formulate them into the Deuteronomic programme of revival. In so doing they dissociated it from the monarchy, chiefly on account of the reactionary policies of Jehoahaz and Jehoiakim, and founded it upon the authority of Moses.[7]

One initial difficulty raised by this theory concerns the law book which was discovered in the Temple in Josiah's reign. That such a book was found is clearly accepted by Bächli for he bases part of his thesis concerning the functions of the monarchy upon the record in 2 Kings xxiii. 2 of Josiah's reading of the book of the law before the people.[8] But on the hypothesis presented here this law book cannot have been Deuteronomy which was not composed until after Josiah's death. What role then did the book play in the reformation? Even Bächli agrees that it contributed something. But if this

[1] Ibid., pp. 196f.
[2] Ibid., pp. 203ff.
[3] G. von Rad, *Old Testament Theology* I (1962), pp. 334ff.
[4] O. Bächli, op. cit., p. 199.
[5] Ibid., pp. 203f.
[6] Ibid., pp. 200f.
[7] Ibid., pp. 201–202.
[8] Ibid., p. 188.

is so then Josiah's enactments cannot be attributed solely to his own political and cultic desires; they were also stimulated by the demands of the newly discovered book. And if this is accepted then surely the most reasonable position to adopt is that this book was, as the narrative in 2 Kings obviously indicates, Deuteronomy and that the demands of this book stand in a large measure behind the reformation, especially in its cultic aspects. Bächli's theory clearly leaves little or no room for the influence of the law book upon the reformation and indeed implies that it afterwards fell into oblivion and was lost. It also involves regarding the narrative in Kings in so far as it would identify the law book with Deuteronomy as pure fiction, a view which we have seen at an earlier stage in our discussion to be highly improbable.

In addition to this objection it must be questioned if Bächli is correct in believing Deuteronomy to have been influenced by the Jerusalem ideology of kingship. That the king did play an important role in the cult and in the administration of the law is commonly agreed. That he was the centre of political power can hardly be disputed. But these are not the marks which distinguish the Judaean monarchy from its northern counterpart. Jeroboam I is a clear example of a non-Davidic king exercising such political and cultic functions. What does distinguish the Davidic monarchy from the northern is the unique theological traditions which surrounded it, the basis of which was the notion of a special covenant between Yahweh and the house of David.[1] This covenant tradition seems to have emerged soon after David had captured the old Jebusite stronghold of Jerusalem and made it his capital. Its beginnings can be seen already in the oracle of Nathan to David (2 Sam. vii. 8f. esp. 11b.–16):[2]

> 'Moreover the Lord declares to you that the Lord will make you a house. When your days are fulfilled and you lie down with your fathers, I will raise up your offspring after you, who shall come forth from your body, and I will establish his kingdom. . . I will be his father, and he shall be my son . . . And your house and your kingdom shall be made sure for ever before me; your throne shall be established for ever.'

Similarly, the so-called 'last words of David' assert:

> 'Yea, does not my house stand so with God?
> For he has made with me an everlasting covenant,
> ordered in all things and secure.

[1] For this see A. R. Johnson, *Sacral Kingship in Ancient Israel* (Cardiff, 1955).

[2] For a discussion of Nathan's oracle see R. E. Clements, *Prophecy and Covenant*, (London, 1965), pp. 56ff.

For will he not cause to prosper all my help and my desire?'

(2 Sam. xxiii. 5)

From these beginnings there developed in Jerusalem a covenant tradition which overlaid to a large extent the older Sinai traditions upon which Deuteronomy is based. That is not to say that the Jerusalem cult tradition did not preserve certain features of the older tradition. There is considerable evidence to show that it did.[1] But the Davidic covenant traditions eventually took precedence over the older Sinai tradition and developed it in such a manner as to alter its normative form and reduce it to a secondary position in the Jerusalem cult.[2] In view of this it is impossible to regard Deuteronomy as an expression of specifically Jerusalem traditions. Not only is it founded upon the older Sinai covenant traditions with no mention of the later Davidic traditions, but its polemical attitude towards kingship and the strict limitations which it places upon the monarchy rule out quite decisively any possibility of its origin among Jerusalem circles. This is further evidenced when it is remembered that the original book in all probability had even less to say about kingship than the present book.[3] There is reason to believe that those verses which stipulate the duty of the king towards the book of the law (Deut. xvii. 18f.) may be the work of the Deuteronomistic historian who was here formulating one of the standards, indeed the main standard, by which he judges the monarchy in the book of Kings, viz. the solemn obligation laid upon the king to observe all the demands of the law of Moses.[4]

On the basis of our discussion thus far it is clear that any theory of a purely northern or Judaean provenance of Deuteronomy cannot be accepted as a satisfactory solution to the problem on hand. On the one hand, any theory of a purely northern origin of the book, as represented by the work of Alt and Dumermuth, fails to deal

[1] Cf. R. E. Clements, ibid., pp. 63f.

[2] For the relationship between the Sinai covenant traditions and the Davidic covenant traditions see R. E. Clements, ibid., pp. 56ff.

[3] *Contra* Bächli (op. cit., p. 202) who suggests that Deuteronomy may indeed have at one time said more about monarchy than in its present form.

[4] Even if the law of the king (Deut. xvii. 14–20) be ascribed in its entirety to *Urdeuteronomium*, we cannot agree with Bächli (op. cit., pp. 88f., 187) in interpreting verse 19 as referring to the public reading of the law by the king. This verse refers rather to the king's own personal duty to read the law in order that he himself will learn to fear the Lord, etc. Cf. W. L. Moran's remarks on this in his review of Bächli's book in *Biblica* 44 (1963), p. 377. On the law of the king in Deut. xvii. 14f. see G. von Rad, *Deuteronomium*, pp. 85f. where it is suggested that verses 18–19 are later additions to the original law.

with the question of how such a northern reformation programme found its way to Jerusalem and was there accepted and enforced by the Judaean authorities. On the other hand, theories of a specifically Judaean provenance, as advocated in the works of von Rad and Bächli, fail to explain the marked affinities between the book and north Israelite traditions and literature. The initial problem therefore remains: how are we to account for Deuteronomy's northern background and at the same time its acceptance and application by the Judaean authorities?

The thesis we wish to advance here is that Deuteronomy originated among a northern circle who fled south to Judah after the destruction of the northern kingdom in 721 B.C. and there formulated their old traditions into a programme of reform and revival which they intended to be carried out by the Judaean authorities with whom they believed the future of Israel to lie. In composing their work the authors had in mind Jerusalem as the cultic and political centre of the reformation movement and made certain concessions to the Jerusalem cult tradition. Such a view would obviously present a plausible solution to the problem for it would account for Deuteronomy's north Israelite background as well as its presence in Jerusalem in Josiah's reign.

Several considerations lend their support to such a theory. Perhaps the most important concerns the law of the sanctuary in Deuteronomy. We have already seen that there are no sound grounds for calling in question the view that Deuteronomy demands the centralization of worship to one sole sanctuary and that this forms one of the fundamental characteristics of the book. Few today would dispute this. There is, however, considerable disagreement concerning the origin of this demand and the identity of the sanctuary in the minds of those who formulated it in Deuteronomy. G. Hölscher, for example, argued that it was nothing more than the utopian and completely impracticable ideal of a group of priests living in exile and divorced from the realities of life in Palestine where, it is contended, such a law would have been impossible to enforce.[1] Such a view must be rejected for two major reasons. In the first place there is no sound reason for rejecting as unhistorical the narratives concerning the attempt of both Hezekiah (2 Kings xviii. 4, 22) and Josiah (2 Kings xxiii. 8) to centralize the cult. And secondly,

[1] G. Hölscher, 'Komposition und Ursprung des Deuteronomiums', *ZAW* 40 (1922), pp. 183ff. and *Geschichte der israelitischen und jüdischen Religion* (Giessen, 1922), pp. 132f. Hölscher detects several idealistic and what he believes to be impracticable features in Deuteronomy.

the law of one sanctuary far from being impracticable became eventually one of the basic features of Judaism in the post-exilic period onwards.[1] A. Bentzen has suggested that the centralization law was the final outcome of a long process in which the larger and more important sanctuaries monopolized so much of the offerings of the people that the smaller local shrines suffered an ever-increasing loss of revenue as a result of which their priests legislated that worship should be concentrated at one of the major sanctuaries with a view to having themselves accepted into the ministry there.[2] Several objections may be raised against this. Firstly, whilst it is probably true that the larger sanctuaries such as Bethel and Jerusalem would have attracted many pilgrims from all over the land, there is no evidence whatsoever that this had adverse effects on the revenues or status of the rural shrines. Indeed the fact that Deuteronomy militates so strongly against them and that in spite of Hezekiah's and Josiah's attempt to destroy them they persistently sprang up again would seem to indicate that they were far from being robbed of their popularity among the people or that they suffered any great loss in income. Furthermore, the fact that Deuteronomy itself over and over again insists on charity towards the country levites who were now to be deprived of their altars is surely evidence that such altars had hitherto provided the means of livelihood for these priests. Recently it has been suggested that the demand for the central shrine has its origin in the central shrine which we now know to have been a characteristic of the amphictyonic period.[3] But this is not satisfactory for it fails to distinguish between the amphictyonic shrine as the main cultic centre among a multiplicity of local sanctuaries and the Deuteronomic demand for one and only one place of worship for all Israel.

It seems to the present writer that the simplest solution to this problem is to interpret the centralization law in Deuteronomy as referring to Jerusalem and as having its origin within the context of the Jerusalem cult traditions.[4] Recent research has shown quite clearly that these traditions were based upon two fundamental

[1] Cf. C. R. North, 'Pentateuchal Criticism' in *OTMS* (ed. H. H. Rowley, Oxford, 1951), p. 50; W. C. Graham 'The Modern Controversy about Deuteronomy', *JR* 7 (1927), p. 415; K. Budde, 'Das Deuteronomium und die Reform König Josias', *ZAW* 44 (1926), pp. 179f.

[2] A. Bentzen, *Die josianische Reform und ihre Voraussetzungen* (Copenhagen, 1926), pp. 68–72.

[3] Cf. for example, J. Bright, *A History of Israel*, p. 265; F. Dumermuth, op. cit., p. 62.

[4] Cf. R. E. Clements, 'Deuteronomy and the Jerusalem Cult Tradition,' *VT* 15 (1965), pp. 300–312.

theological principles, viz. Yahweh's choice of Mount Zion for his dwelling-place and his choice of David and his successors as his anointed king and ruler of Israel.[1] It was Jerusalem which claimed a unique and special relationship with Yahweh and, even more significant, it was in Jerusalem that the first attempt at centralization of worship was made. As far as we know it was Hezekiah who first made such an innovation.[2] His motives for doing so are not clearly known to us but it is possible that they were largely political and sprang from his desire to re-establish the political and cultic centrality of Jerusalem, perhaps particularly against the claims of Bethel, in his attempt to regain possession of the territory of the northern kingdom and to establish once again the 'all Israel' state of the Davidic-Solomonic period.[3] Whatever his motives were, however, it is clear that we have here the first attempt to exalt the claims of one sanctuary to the complete exclusion of all others. In view of this it is hardly a coincidence that at a slightly later period a book made its appearance in Jerusalem which contained a formulation of a law demanding precisely what Hezekiah had attempted to do in the cultic sphere. Here surely the most reasonable conclusion is that in their law of the sanctuary the authors of Deuteronomy were giving expression to the traditional primacy of Jerusalem and lending their support and indeed in their book claiming Mosaic authority for the innovation made by Hezekiah. It is significant too that in formulating the centralization law they employed a terminology which we have reason to believe was used in the Jerusalem traditions to describe Yahweh's choice of Mount Zion.[4] As in these traditions Yahweh was believed to have chosen (*bāḥar*) Mount Zion, so also in Deuteronomy it is legislated that Yahweh will choose (*bāḥar*) a place in which to make his name dwell. This is not to say of course that the Deuteronomic circle accepted the traditional claims of Mount Zion in their entirety. It is clear that they accorded no room to the belief that Yahweh himself dwelt in the sanctuary; only his name dwelt on earth. Nor did

[1] Cf. for example, H.-J. Kraus, *Die Königsherrschaft Gottes im Alten Testament* (Tübingen, 1951) and *Worship in Israel* (Oxford, 1966), pp. 179ff.

[2] 2 Chron. xiv. 1–4 and xvii. 6 both claim that Asa and Jehoshaphat respectively abolished the high places. That these statements are historically untrustworthy is clear from the fact that the Chronicler himself contradicts them (cf. 2 Chron. xvi. 17 and xx. 33) as also does the author of Kings (1 Kings xv. 14 and xxii. 43).

[3] For this see my article, 'The Centralization of the Cult in Deuteronomy', *VT* 13 (1963), pp. 380–389.

[4] Cf. R. E. Clements, 'Deuteronomy and the Jerusalem Cult Tradition', *VT* 15 (1965), pp. 303–304 and his *God and Temple* (Oxford, 1965), pp. 48f., following K. Koch, 'Zur Geschichte der Erwählungsvorstellung in Israel', *ZAW* 67 (1955), pp. 205ff.

they see the uniqueness of Jerusalem as in any way related to the ideology surrounding the Davidic monarchy. The centralization of the cult was probably accepted by them simply in the interests of cultic purity and as a means of countering the widespread syncretism which had pervaded the rural shrines.[1] There is no reason to doubt therefore that Josiah was correct in interpreting the centralization law in Deuteronomy as referring to his own capital and that the author of Kings was also correct in doing likewise. Here then we have evidence that the authors of Deuteronomy though coming ultimately from northern Israel drew up their programme of reform in Jerusalem and with Jerusalem in mind as the cult centre of the revival movement which they envisaged and hoped for.

One other piece of evidence in favour of this view emerges from Deuteronomy's peculiar election terminology to which some reference has already been made.[2] We have seen that as far as the Old Testament documents are concerned Deuteronomy is the first to employ the word *bāḥar* ('to choose') to define what Yahweh had done for Israel in the exodus event.[3] Here we have the first formal expression in the literature of the Old Testament of the doctrine of election which was implicit in Israel's faith from the beginning.

From where did the authors of Deuteronomy derive this distinctive election terminology? It could be argued that they themselves were responsible for it. Or it is possible that G. E. Mendenhall is correct in seeing it as originating among a now unknown circle from whom the Deuteronomic party derived it,[4] although R. E. Clements has correctly pointed out that there is no evidence at all to support such a view.[5] Clements himself has recently made what seems to the present writer to be the most plausible solution to this problem by tracing the origin of this election terminology to the ideology of the Davidic monarchy in Jerusalem.[6] Following the suggestion of G. Quell and S. Amsler,[7] he argues that the verb *bāḥar* was in use from the time of David onwards to describe the belief in Yahweh's choice of David and his successors to be his anointed rulers over all Israel

[1] R. E. Clements, 'Deuteronomy and the Jerusalem Cult Tradition', *VT* 15 (1965), p. 304.

[2] For what follows I am indebted to R. E. Clements who has made the suggestion in the article referred to the previous footnote.

[3] See above pp. 56f.

[4] G. E. Mendenhall, 'Election', *IDB*, II (1962), p. 79.

[5] R. E. Clements, 'Deuteronomy and the Jerusalem Cult Tradition', *VT* 15 (1965), p. 305.

[6] Ibid., pp. 305f.

[7] G. Quell, 'Die Erwählung im A.T.', *ThWzNT* IV, p. 163; S. Amsler, *David, Roi et Messie* (Neuchatel, 1963), pp. 39f., 77.

and that the authors of Deuteronomy adopted this terminology and applied it to Yahweh's election of Israel as his peculiar people.[1] Clements sees here a polemical attitude on the part of the authors of Deuteronomy towards the Jerusalem ideology of kingship: 'Instead of proclaiming the sacral foundation of the Israelite state in terms of the divine election of its monarchy, the Deuteronomists declared that what Yahweh had elected was a people for his own possession, and that it was merely by a concession that this people were themselves allowed to elect a king from among their number'.[2] Clements in fact detects an attitude of censure in Deuteronomy towards not only the monarchy but also towards other aspects of the Jerusalem cult tradition. To what extent such a view is tenable will be discussed presently. Here, however, there is every reason to believe that he is correct in his suggestion concerning the origin of Deuteronomy's election terminology. It is, as he himself argues,[3] a more scientific proceeding to explain the background of this language from a tradition which clearly did exist, than to postulate, as for example Mendenhall does, the existence of an esoteric group of which we have no evidence whatsoever. Here then we have further evidence of the influence of the Jerusalem traditions upon the authors of Deuteronomy. They formulated their own distinctive concept of Yahweh's election of Israel using the terminology employed to describe his choice of the Davidic monarchy in the Jerusalem traditions.

The thesis here presented that the circle responsible for Deuteronomy though originating in northern Israel had fled south to Judah after 721 B.C. and there drew up their programme of reform and revival with Jerusalem as its political and cultic centre is further substantiated by a consideration of the historical background of its appearance in Jerusalem in 621 B.C.

The collapse and destruction of the northern kingdom in 721 B.C. had evidently far-reaching effects in Judah. On the one hand there seems to have been a quick realization among the authorities there that here at last was the opportunity to extend the borders of the southern kingdom to include the territory of the northern provinces and to re-unite the people and establish once more the pre-disruption all-Israel state. Alongside this and as its complement there developed a movement for cultic and religious reformation which no doubt originated among Yahwistic circles who saw the calamity which had befallen the northern people as Yahweh's judgment upon their

[1] R. E. Clements, 'Deuteronomy and the Jerusalem Cult Tradition', *VT* 15 (1965), pp. 306f. [2] Ibid., p. 306. [3] Ibid., p. 306.

apostasy and idolatry and who wished to avoid a similar fate for Judah. Hence there arose in Judah in the late eighth century a movement which aimed at both political and religious renewal.

Such a movement stands behind the reformation and rebellion of Hezekiah in whose reign the first opportunity for realizing its aims arose. It seems to have come in 705 B.C. when the Assyrian overlord Sargon died and his successor Sennacherib was met on his accession to the throne by widespread rebellion throughout his empire.[1] Hezekiah, who appears to have been the ringleader of revolt in the west, did not let the opportunity pass by. On the political level he rejected the Assyrian suzerainty of Judah and took steps to extend his borders. The narrative in Kings states that he moved against the Philistine territory to the west (2 Kings xviii. 8) whilst 2 Chronicles xxx. 1f., however much coloured by the later Samaritan schism, is undoubtedly trustworthy in recording his attempt to win the allegiance of the northern tribes.[2] At the same time he carried out certain reforms in the cultic sphere, the most notable being the centralization of worship to Jerusalem. These reforms would also have included the abolition of the Assyrian cultic emblems from the Temple precincts. This together with the centralization of the cult may have been motivated to some degree by political aims[3] although it can hardly be doubted that with the other cultic innovations and changes noted in 2 Kings xviii. 4f. they also gave expression to the desire for religious renewal and reform abroad at the time.

Hezekiah's rebellion and reformation were, however, short-lived for Sennacherib quickly regained control and in 701 B.C. marched west to subdue the rebels and re-establish the Assyrian hegemony. In Manasseh's reign there was a radical reaction against his father's policy. Once more the local shrines flourished and various pagan cults seem to have been practised in the Temple itself (cf. 2 Kings xxi. 7; xxiii. 4–7; Zeph. i. 4). But the desire for reform and national independence lived on and, as we have seen, in Josiah's reign when the Assyrian power finally began to crumble the movement reasserted itself.

It is against this background that the origin of Deuteronomy is to

[1] Cf. H. W. F. Saggs, *The Greatness that was Babylon* (London, 1962), pp. 118f.; J. Bright, *A History of Israel*, p. 276.

[2] Cf. J. Bright, *A History of Israel*, p. 266. It has been suggested that Hezekiah's Passover celebration followed a north Israelite calendar. Cf. H.-J. Kraus, 'Zur Geschichte des Passah-Massot-Festes im Alten Testament', *EvTh* 18 (1958), pp. 47–67.

[3] Cf. my article 'The Centralization of the Cult in Deuteronomy' *VT* 13 (1963), pp. 380–389.

be viewed. After 721 B.C. it must have been clear that the future of Israel lay in Judah which had survived the devastation wrought by the Assyrians upon the northern kingdom. The Judaean authorities themselves soon realized this. But it would have been equally clear to circles of northerners who had fled south in and after 721 B.C. that any real possibility of revival both political and religious within the nation as a whole now rested with the Judaean powers. That this was so was soon given concrete expression in Hezekiah's religious and political enactments. It was in this situation that the Deuteronomic circle saw their opportunity. Hezekiah's aims were basically identical with their own, that is, national independence and revival and the purification of Israel's worship of Yahweh. The difference would have lain mainly in the position to be occupied by the Davidic monarchy and the sacral traditions of the Jerusalem cult in such a revival movement. These traditions were fundamentally foreign to the covenant concepts of the Deuteronomic circle. In an attempt to overcome this obstacle the authors of Deuteronomy made certain concessions to these traditions. They formulated their own distinctive traditions into a programme of reformation which was to have its centre in Jerusalem itself. In so doing they adopted Hezekiah's claims for the exclusive centrality of the Temple for Israel's cult and gave it nothing less than the authority of the 'law of Moses' (Deut. xii, etc.). At the same time they employed the familiar election terminology of the Mount Zion ideology to describe the place which Yahweh would choose. Similarly, they appropriated the same terminology employed in Jerusalem to define Yahweh's choice of David and used it to describe their own doctrine of his election of Israel to be his peculiar people. Even in the law of the king itself it is perhaps not without significance that this same election language is used—Yahweh would *choose* a king for his people (Deut. xvii. 15)—although of course this must not be seen as any acceptance of the Davidic kingship ideology. All this is to be regarded, in the writer's opinion, as the attempt of the Deuteronomic circle to gain acceptance for their reform programme by the Jerusalem authorities. But such concessions in no way compromised their own basic theological traditions. Nowhere in Deuteronomy, it must be repeated, is there any place accorded to the sacral kingship ideology surrounding the house of David whilst the acceptance of the centrality of Jerusalem is indeed in itself no real concession since it would almost certainly have been regarded by the authors of the book as a vital means of securing the cultic purity for which they strove.

The thesis here presented then is that the Deuteronomic circle living in Judah after 721 B.C. onwards made a conscious effort to integrate their own reformation and revival plans into those envisaged and attempted by Hezekiah. They must be seen therefore as having composed Deuteronomy after this king's abortive reformation and not, as has sometimes been held, before it.[1] In drawing up their programme they have embodied some of the basic principles of Hezekiah's reformation though at the same time orientating them towards their own particular theological traditions. The marked similarities between Hezekiah's policies and enactments and the demands of Deuteronomy further support this theory. The king attempted to re-unite Israel and to concentrate the national cult in Jerusalem. Deuteronomy too aims at binding together the 'people of Yahweh' and uncompromisingly demands the centralization of worship to one sanctuary. Hezekiah's struggle for independence and the nationalistic movement in the seventh century in Judah are more than echoed in Deuteronomy's concern for Israel's existence among foreign peoples.

The precise period in which Deuteronomy was composed was very probably during Manasseh's reign.[2] At this time the Assyrian power was at its strongest under the able Asshur-ban-apal (*c.* 669–633 B.C.) and would have evoked a correspondingly strong desire for national independence among loyal Judaean circles. In addition it was a time of widespread apostasy and idolatry which would clearly have augmented the need for religious renewal and cultic purity. There was also evidently bitter persecution of loyal Yahwistic circles (cf. 2 Kings xxi. 16). Once again it was the prophets who raised their voice in protest and condemnation (2 Kings xxi. 10f.) and in view of what we have already concluded concerning the prophetic origins of Deuteronomy it is not impossible that it was within the ranks of these prophets that its authors are to be found.

The Deuteronomic party therefore probably worked during these dark days under Manasseh and drew up their book in the

[1] Such a view was advocated by some older critics such as E. Sellin, *Introduction to the Old Testament* (E.T. from the 3rd German edit., London, 1923), pp. 73f. (In the 6th edition of this work (1933) Sellin abandoned such a view in favour of a date for the composition of Deuteronomy shortly before its discovery under Josiah in 621 B.C.) More recently H. Junker, 'Die Entstehungszeit des Ps. 78 und das Deuteronomium', *Biblica* 34 (1953), pp. 487–500 has restated the same view.

[2] Older commentators such as S. R. Driver, Robertson Smith, Kittel, Siebens, Oesterley and Robinson favoured this date. At present it is favoured by H. H. Rowley, 'The Prophet Jeremiah and the Book of Deuteronomy', in *From Moses to Qumran* (1963), p. 195; G. E. Wright, *Deuteronomy, IB*, II (1953), p. 323.

hope that some time in the future the dawn would break and there would once more be, as in Hezekiah's reign, an opportunity for reformation. We now know that that opportunity presented itself under Josiah who had evidently the same intentions as Hezekiah had a century or so before. It was, as we have seen, during the course of Josiah's enactments that Deuteronomy was discovered and its demands enforced by the king. It is rather tempting indeed to suggest that when the authors of Deuteronomy realized Josiah's intentions to revive Hezekiah's policies they deposited the book in the Temple in the hope that it would be conveniently discovered there and accepted by the Judaean authorities. But there is no proof that they did so. Whatever the circumstances surrounding these events may have been, however, the book was eventually discovered and was accepted by the Judaean reforming party and used by them to supplement their own reform measures which were already in process of being carried out.

Here then we have a plausible solution to the immediate origin of Deuteronomy. We may summarize it as follows. After 721 B.C. the Deuteronomic circle fled south to Judah in the belief that the possible future religious and political revival of the nation lay there. Such a belief was soon confirmed when Hezekiah inaugurated and attempted to carry out such a revival. When this attempt ultimately failed and reaction set in under Manasseh they drew up their own plans for reformation in the form of Deuteronomy. In order to have it accepted and put into operation by the Judaean authorities they made certain concessions to the Jerusalem traditions notably in demanding the centralization of the cult. When Josiah came to the throne and the Assyrian power began to decline the aims of Hezekiah were revived. In the course of this revival in Josiah's reign the book was discovered in the Temple where it had been deposited by its authors. It was accepted by the authorities in Jerusalem and became the basis for further reformation enactments which supplemented those already enforced by them.

Such a theory presents a satisfactory solution to the many-sided problem of the origin of Deuteronomy. It accounts for the northern background of the basic traditions underlying the book and at the same time explains how it came to be in Jerusalem in the late seventh century B.C. It offers also an explanation of why it was necessary for its authors to deposit it in the Temple. They themselves as a non-Judaean circle had not the power to implement its demands and acknowledged that the only satisfactory means of achieving this was to attempt to have it accepted and enforced by those who had that power, the Jerusalem authorities.

The thesis here presented agrees to some extent with the views recently advanced by R. E. Clements to which reference has already been made.[1] Clements too acknowledges that some attempt must be made to explain how such a stream of northern traditions as is contained in Deuteronomy arrived in Jerusalem and was there accepted and enforced by the Judaean authorities.[2] His solution to this problem is that the authors of Deuteronomy had come south to Judah after 721 B.C. and composed their work in Jerusalem intending it to lead to a reform of the Jerusalem cult tradition. He detects four ways in which they have attempted to do this. The first concerns the manner in which the Ark is treated in the book (Deut. x. 1–5; xxxi. 9, 25f.). In the Jerusalem traditions the Ark was the throne of the invisibly present Yahweh whose dwelling-place was Mount Zion. To the Deuteronomic circle such a view was unacceptable; Yahweh dwells in heaven and only his name is present in the sanctuary. Accordingly in Deuteronomy the Ark is merely the container of the tables of the law. That is, it has, to use von Rad's phrase, been 'demythologized'[3] and robbed of its ancient mystique as the Cherubim-throne of God. Thus, according to Clements, the authors of Deuteronomy have here attempted to re-interpret the significance of the Ark and to reform the Jerusalem attitude towards it.[4] The second piece of evidence adduced by Clements concerns the law of the sanctuary. Here, it is argued, the Deuteronomic party are conceding and even extending the old claim of Jerusalem to a position of primacy. But they did so with two major alterations. They denied that Mount Zion was Yahweh's dwelling-place in the old mythico-cultic sense by setting forth the doctrine that only his name dwelt there. And secondly, they dissociated the uniqueness of the sanctuary from the political claims of the Davidic monarchy.[5] Thus there is here, it is contended, a note of censure not only against the traditional claims of Mount Zion but also against the Jerusalem ideology of kingship. Such a polemical attitude towards the monarchy is further detected, in Clements's opinion, in the Deuteronomic formulation of Israel's election. Here, he contends, the authors of Deuteronomy have employed the terminology used to describe Yahweh's

[1] R. E. Clements, 'Deuteronomy and the Jerusalem Cult Tradition', *VT* 15 (1965), pp. 300–312.
[2] Ibid., p. 301.
[3] G. von Rad, *Studies in Deuteronomy*, p. 40.
[4] R. E. Clements, 'Deuteronomy and the Jerusalem Cult Tradition', *VT* 15 (1965), pp. 301–303.
[5] Ibid., pp. 303–305.

election of David and his successors and have applied it instead to his election of all Israel probably as a deliberate counterbalance to the excessive claims of the Jerusalem kingship theology.[1] Finally, it is argued that the particular significance which Deuteronomy attaches to the idea of Yahweh's land which he had given to his people is aimed at opposing the Jerusalem doctrine that Mount Zion was especially the symbol of Yahweh's holy land, a doctrine which reflects the ancient near eastern notion which relates the cult of a sacred mountain to the divine ownership of the land in which it was located.[2] Against such a mythico-cultic doctrine, Clements argues, Deuteronomy asserts a 'historical' tradition which expresses the belief that Yahweh had providentially ordered the events of history and had enabled Israel to drive out the indigenous peoples of Canaan and to take possession of it as her inheritance. There is here no hint of any kind of cultic bond uniting Yahweh with the land.[3]

According to this view, therefore, the authors of Deuteronomy were concerned with reforming the specifically Jerusalem cult tradition, especially in its sacral ideology of Mount Zion and the Davidic monarchy, and in consequence of this they have been influenced by a number of features deriving from these traditions.

In so far as it traces the immediate background of the composition of Deuteronomy to Jerusalem in the seventh century this theory is clearly in agreement with the views advanced by the present writer in the previous pages of this chapter. Furthermore, Clements is surely correct in detecting certain features and characteristics of the Jerusalem cult traditions. It may be questioned, however, if the polemical attitude which he detects in the book is as pronounced or deliberate as his theory suggests. It is probable, for example, that those passages in which the Ark is mentioned (Deut. x. 1–5; xxxi. 9, 25f.) are later additions to the original book.[4] If this is so then clearly they cannot be cited as evidence of a desire on the part of the authors of that book to re-interpret or reform the significance of the Ark in the Jerusalem traditions. That the passages in question do in fact present a non-Jerusalem concept of the Ark is not here disputed. But they were very probably not present in *Urdeuteronomium* and

[1] R. E. Clements, op. cit., pp. 305–307.

[2] For this see R. E. Clements, 'Temple and Land', *TGUOS* 19 (1963), pp. 16–28, esp. pp. 20f. and his later work *God and Temple* (1965), esp. pp. 1f., 50f., 73f.

[3] R. E. Clements, 'Deuteronomy and the Jerusalem Cult Tradition', *VT* 15 (1965), pp. 307f.

[4] See above p. 31.

are probably, as we have seen, the work of the later Deuteronomistic historian.

In the law of kingship (Deut. xvii. 14f.) there is to be sure a polemical element. It is clear that the authors of Deuteronomy regarded monarchy as a foreign institution introduced into Israel through her desire to be 'like all the nations that are round about' (Deut. xvii. 14). Yet even here one may ask if this attitude is directed specifically against the Davidic monarchy or against monarchy in general. There is considerable evidence in the Old Testament to indicate that right from the beginning kingship was regarded in some circles with a certain amount of misgiving. But it seems that even the prophetic party in the northern kingdom, who were at times its bitterest opponents, were realistic enough to see that when monarchy was introduced into Israel it had come to stay. Accordingly they accepted the *status quo* but subject to strict control and limitations. It is against such a background that we must view the law of the king in Deuteronomy. Here too there is an implied acknowledgment that monarchy was a permanent part of Israel's life; it was an integral aspect of the political *status quo*. It is therefore legislated that Israel may have a king but that he would rule under the sufferance of Yahweh who would *choose* him. Whilst the authors of the book were not willing to compromise their own negative attitude towards kingship, is it not possible that in using this election terminology (*bāḥar*) they intended the Judaean monarchy to interpret it in the light of the Jerusalem tradition of Yahweh's *choice* of David? If, as we have suggested, they were attempting to have their book accepted and enforced by that monarchy as a programme of reformation then such a possibility cannot be ruled out.

In view of all this, is it really possible to see the motive behind the composition of Deuteronomy as its authors' desire to reform the Jerusalem cult tradition? Is it conceivable that in the period in which the book was composed, when the northern kingdom had been swept away and the southern state had reached its lowest point from both a political and religious point of view, its authors had such a relatively narrow intention? Is it not more probable that, as we have suggested, these men had a more pressing urgency on their minds—the survival of their people? It was a time for reviving the nation in the face of political and religious disintegration when Israel's existence as Yahweh's covenant people was threatened with nothing less than extinction. This surely is the real motive behind the composition of Deuteronomy. Those responsible for it had come south after the catastrophe of 721 B.C.

in the belief that the future of the nation as a whole lay with Judah. Working in Jerusalem they formulated their own traditions into a reformation programme which they hoped would some time be accepted and carried out by the Judaean authorities. In so doing they were, as we have seen, influenced by certain aspects of the Jerusalem traditions and in one major point—the centralization of worship—made a concession to those traditions. Their hopes were fulfilled when eventually Josiah came to the throne and Deuteronomy was accorded a major role in the reform movement of his reign.

The immediate background to the composition of Deuteronomy is therefore Jerusalem in the seventh century B.C. Here the prophetic circles who had come south after 721 B.C. and who with their predecessors in the northern kingdom were the custodians of the old amphictyonic traditions underlying the book worked during the reign of Manasseh and drew up their plans for reviving and reforming the nation when the opportunity for doing so would arise. When this did happen the book of Deuteronomy entered a new phase in its history and became the basis of an attempt to interpret from a theological point of view the history of Israel from Moses to the exile. This attempt is contained in the corpus Deuteronomy–2 Kings and represents the work of the Deuteronomistic historian. Since certain aspects of this work are of importance for the discussion of the origin and authorship of Deuteronomy with which we have been concerned, we must now turn to a brief consideration of it.

CHAPTER VI

DEUTERONOMY AND THE DEUTERONOMIST

ONE of the most important contributions to our study of the Old Testament during the past generation is M. Noth's thesis, already referred to on several occasions in the course of our investigation, that the corpus Deuteronomy–2 Kings is not the final outcome of a process of literary redaction and expansion of an original work or series of works, but represents the attempt of an author to write the history of Israel from Moses to the exile and to interpret that history from a theological standpoint.[1] This Deuteronomistic historian wrote in the shadow of 721 B.C. and 586 B.C. and was concerned with explaining how the catastrophes which befell Israel in these years came about. The fundamental position adopted is that down through the centuries Israel had continually and increasingly failed to obey the will of Yahweh as revealed in the 'law of Moses', that is, Deuteronomy, until he finally rejected her, the northern kingdom in 721 B.C. and the southern in 586 B.C. The author of this work had at his disposal a great deal of material deriving from very varied sources and periods in Israel's history all of which he has knit together into a structural unity by means of a literary framework which together with frequent insertions and comments set forth his own theological interpretation of the events he records.

It is not our purpose here to examine this history work in all its aspects or to enter into a discussion of the various questions raised by Noth's theory. What we are concerned with is an attempt to determine the relationship between the author of this work and the authors of Deuteronomy and to see if this has any relevance for the conclusions arrived at above concerning the origin of Deuteronomy itself.

The general impression conveyed by studies in this question is that there is a gap not only in time but in standpoint between the circles responsible for Deuteronomy and the Deuteronomistic author or authors.[2] The usual view seems to be that the book of Deuteronomy

[1] M. Noth, *Überlieferungsgeschichtliche Studien I*² (Tübingen, 1957).

[2] Even if, with Noth, we believe that the work is from the pen of an individual rather than a group of authors, he must nevertheless be seen as representing a circle of tradition.

having been discovered in the Jerusalem Temple where it had been deposited by its authors was then adopted and cherished by another and different circle and eventually employed by them in writing their history. This Deuteronomistic circle was not only strongly influenced in both language and theology by Deuteronomy itself, however, but also by the specifically Jerusalem traditions concerning Yahweh's choice of Mount Zion as his dwelling-place and the house of David to be his anointed rulers over Israel. Thus it is commonly agreed that in the Deuteronomistic history there is a fusion of two originally separate blocks of tradition, the Sinai/Mosaic traditions and the Mount Zion/Davidic traditions.[1] The author of this history is therefore considered as belonging exclusively neither to one nor the other of these individual traditions but as standing as it were mid-way between them deriving his theological standpoint from certain aspects of both of them.[2]

It is this view that we wish to challenge and to attempt to show that whilst the Deuteronomistic circle has certainly been influenced by specifically Jerusalem traditions there is a more direct relationship between it and the circles responsible for Deuteronomy and that both in fact belong ultimately to the same basic stream of tradition.

The first piece of evidence to substantiate this view lies in the remarkable similarity in language and style between Deuteronomy and the Deuteronomist. We have already had occasion to examine the contribution of the Deuteronomist to the growth of Deuteronomy itself and the strong possibility has emerged that considerable portions of the present book come from his pen, particularly the first introduction in chapters i–iii (iv) and parts of the last four chapters (xxxi. 1–13, 24–26a, xxxiv) as well as the plural passages within chapters v–xxx.[3] Indeed it is precisely here that the greatest difficulty in discussing the growth of Deuteronomy has arisen for there is a striking homogeneity in style throughout the entire book with the exception of only a few short passages. It is mainly this which has given rise to the wide diversity of opinion, to which attention has been drawn, among scholars on the question of what parts of the present book belonged to *Urdeuteronomium* and what parts are subsequent additions and expansions.

The two styles, that of Deuteronomy and that of the Deutero-

[1] Cf. G. von Rad, *Old Testament Theology*, I (London, 1962), pp. 334ff.
[2] Ibid., p. 336 footnote 5.
[3] See above pp. 26ff.

nomist, are basically identical. The differences amount to no more than an occasional variation in vocabulary or short phrase and minor nuances in syntax. In view of this it can only be concluded that this unity of style belongs equally to both circles, the Deuteronomic and the Deuteronomistic. We cannot here be dealing with an original Deuteronomic style which has been adopted and slavishly copied by the Deuteronomistic circle which worked at a later period in Israel's history. There is enough similarity between the two works to show a common mode of expression and enough differences to show the natural amount of development which would have arisen during the period which separates the appearance of the two works. The only reasonable conclusion is surely that the Deuteronomist inherited this style from the authors of Deuteronomy directly. In other words, he belongs to the same circle of tradition in which this book originated. He is perfectly at home, so to speak, with this style, using it freely and with ease. It was his own natural mode of expressing himself and not, if one may repeat it, a slavish or cumbersome copying of the style of a book which was originally quite foreign to him.

Further evidence to substantiate this view is to be found in a consideration of the basic theological tradition of the Deuteronomist. It has already been noted that in the Deuteronomistic history work there is a confluence and fusion of two originally separate sets of tradition, the Sinai/Mosaic covenant traditions and the Davidic covenant traditions. The former, represented in the book of Deuteronomy, are based upon Yahweh's election of Israel in the events of exodus and stem from the Sinai covenant ceremony. The latter, on the other hand, have at their basis the belief in a special and unique covenant between Yahweh and the house of David and represent a quite specific ideology of kingship which is totally foreign to the older covenant tradition. In the Deuteronomistic history, however, both have been united in the most remarkable manner. Here in several places the covenant between Yahweh and David is linked to the obligation laid upon the king to obey the 'law of Moses'. One or two examples will serve to illustrate this. The first is contained in David's final charge to his son and successor Solomon (1 Kings ii. 1ff.):

> 'When David's time to die drew near, he charged Solomon his son, saying, "I am about to go the way of all the earth. Be strong, and show yourself a man, and keep the charge of the Lord your God, walking in his ways and keeping his statutes, his commandments, his ordinances, and his testimonies, as it is written in the law of Moses, that you may prosper in all that you do and wherever you turn; that the Lord may establish

> his word which he spoke concerning me, saying, 'If your sons take heed to their way, to walk before me in faithfulness with all their heart and with all their soul, there shall not fail you a man on the throne of Israel.'"'

A similar fusion of the two traditions is also found in Yahweh's words to Solomon after the dedication of the Temple (1 Kings ix. 4f.):

> 'And as for you, if you will walk before me, as David your father walked, with integrity of heart and uprightness, doing according to all that I have commanded you, and keeping my statutes and my ordinances, then I will establish your royal throne over Israel for ever, as I promised David your father, saying, "There shall not fail you a man upon the throne of Israel."'

At the same time attention has been drawn to the many occasions on which the Deuteronomist has portrayed the Davidic kings as appealing to the old traditions concerning Yahweh's election of Israel in the exodus from Egypt and the gift of the promised land (cf. 1 Kings viii. 16, 20f., 34, 36; etc.):[1]

> 'For thou didst separate them from among all the peoples of the earth, to be thy heritage, as thou didst declare through Moses, thy servant, when thou didst bring our fathers out of Egypt, O Lord God.'
>
> (1 Kings viii. 53)

The Deuteronomist was therefore strongly influenced by the Davidic covenant tradition and has arrived at a really exalted concept of the true functions of monarchy, viz. the solemn obligation laid upon the king to conduct his own life according to the demands of the law of Moses and to ensure obedience to it within the nation.[2] This ideal view of monarchy has already been formulated by him in Deuteronomy itself (Deut. xvii. 18f.).[3] Of all the kings of Judah and Israel after David, only Hezekiah (2 Kings xviii. 5–7) and Josiah (2 Kings xxiii. 25) are commended without qualification as having conformed to these requirements.

That the Deuteronomist was also influenced by the Jerusalem traditions concerning the special relationship between Yahweh and Mount Zion is clear from the many allusions to Jerusalem as 'the place which Yahweh has chosen' (1 Kings viii. 16, 44, 48; xi. 13,

[1] Cf. G. von Rad, *Old Testament Theology*, I (1962), pp. 338f.
[2] Ibid., p. 339.
[3] Cf. G. von Rad, *Deuteronomium* (ATD, Göttingen, 1964), pp. 85–86; G. Minette de Tillesse, op. cit., pp. 69–70.

32; xiv. 21; 2 Kings xxi. 7; xxiii. 27). The influence of this tradition must be seen as lying at the basis of his bitter polemic against the northern monarchy in setting up Bethel and Dan as rival sanctuaries to Jerusalem (cf. 1 Kings xii. 26f.; xiii. 1f.; 2 Kings xvii. 7ff.; etc.).

But if this shows evidence of the influence of the Jerusalem cult traditions upon the Deuteronomist, we are left in no doubt as to the primary significance which Deuteronomy had in his thought and of his basic allegiance to its specific theology. This is evident from the fact that for the Deuteronomist the fundamental rule of life for the monarchy is obedience to the 'law of Moses'; the king is to be subject in all things to its requirements and demands. Thus we have here what is best described as a re-interpretation of the Davidic covenant. That covenant seems originally to have been unconditional as is clear from Nathan's oracle to David (2 Sam. vii. 8ff.):

> 'Moreover the Lord declares to you that the Lord will make you a house. When your days are fulfilled and you lie down with your fathers, I will raise up your offspring after you . . . I will be his father, and he shall be my son. When he commits iniquity, I will chasten him with the rod of men, with the stripes of the sons of men; but I will not take my steadfast love from him, as I took it from Saul, whom I put away from before you. And your house and your kingdom shall be made sure for ever before me; your throne shall be established for ever.'
>
> (*vv.* 11b–16)

But in the thought of the Deuteronomist this is no longer so. Here the success and prosperity of David's successors are subject to their faithfulness to the laws of Deuteronomy. That is, the covenant between Yahweh and David is rendered conditional. This is clear from David's last charge to Solomon where Yahweh is recorded as having proclaimed:

> 'If your sons take heed to their way, to walk before me in faithfulness with all their heart and with all their soul, there shall not fail you a man on the throne of Israel.'
>
> (1 Kings ii. 4)

Once again reference may be made to the Deuteronomistic passage in Deuteronomy xvii. 18f. where this conditional nature of the existence of monarchy is expressed:

> 'And when he sits on the throne of his kingdom, he shall write for himself in a book a copy of this law . . . and it shall be with him, and he shall read in it all the days of his life, that he may learn to fear the Lord his

God, by keeping all the words of this law and these statutes, and doing them . . . so that he may continue long in his kingdom, he and his children, in Israel.'[1]

That this view of the conditional nature of the Davidic covenant is rigorously carried through is evidenced by the well-known fact that the Deuteronomist judges each king on the basis of his obedience to the Deuteronomic law, and in particular to the demand for the abolition of the local high places and the centralization of the cult in Jerusalem. Consequently all the kings of the northern state are condemned outright whilst of the kings of Judah only Hezekiah and Josiah are given unqualified praise for having done so.

In this respect therefore the Deuteronomist must be seen as standing within the Deuteronomic tradition. For him the 'law of Moses' is of primary significance and ultimate authority and whilst he is clearly strongly influenced by the Davidic covenant traditions he has re-interpreted them and rendered the continued existence of the Yahweh-David relationship subject to the obedience of the kings to the demands of Deuteronomy. That is to say, he has imposed the conditional nature of the older Sinai covenant between Yahweh and Israel, which could be terminated by Israel's disobedience, upon the Davidic covenant.

Further evidence that the Deuteronomist belongs ultimately to the same tradition as the authors of Deuteronomy comes from the manner in which he has imposed the peculiar Deuteronomic name-theology upon the Mount Zion traditions. The primacy of Jerusalem has been accepted but at the same time re-interpreted. Hence Jerusalem is no longer the city in which Yahweh himself dwells; only his name does so (cf. 1 Kings viii. 29; xiv. 21; 2 Kings xxi. 7; xxiii. 27). By the same token the Jerusalem ideology of the significance of the Ark has been similarly treated. We have already noted the probability that the passages in Deuteronomy (Deut. x. 1–5; xxxi. 9, 25f.) which deal with it derive from the Deuteronomist. Here the Ark has also been subjected to the Deuteronomic name-theology and has been deprived of the significance it had in the Jerusalem cult as the throne of the invisibly present Yahweh. For the Deuteronomist Yahweh's dwelling-place is in heaven. Hence the Ark is conceived by him as nothing more than the receptacle for the tables of the law (cf. further 1 Kings viii. 9, 21). But his attachment to this name-theology is particularly clear in his record of

[1] It is significant that the dynastic principle is accepted here.

Solomon's prayer at the dedication of the Temple (1 Kings viii. 22f., esp. 27f.):

> 'But will God indeed dwell on the earth? Behold, heaven and the highest heaven cannot contain thee; how much less this house which I have built! Yet have regard to the prayer of thy servant and to his supplication, O Lord my God . . . that thy eyes may be open night and day toward this house, the place of which thou hast said, "My name shall be there".'

Here then there is an impressive array of evidence to indicate that the Deuteronomistic historian belongs ultimately to the same circle of tradition as the authors of Deuteronomy. In both language and theological standpoint they are closely related. The difference between them lies in the way in which the Deuteronomist has been influenced by the traditions surrounding the Davidic monarchy. Even here, however, it is clear that there has been no wholesale adoption of these traditions in their specifically Jerusalem form. They have been subjected to the basic theological concepts of the Deuteronomic tradition and in many important aspects radically modified and re-interpreted.

We may summarize the position as follows. The Deuteronomistic history represents the work of a circle who were the direct descendants of the authors of the book of Deuteronomy and who, working in Jerusalem, adopted various aspects of the Jerusalem traditions and re-interpreted them on the basis of their own specific traditions. In this they carried further what had already been done on a lesser scale by the authors of Deuteronomy itself who, as we have seen, adopted and modified certain aspects of the Jerusalem traditions. The book of Deuteronomy and the Deuteronomistic history must therefore be seen as representing two separate phases in the history of the traditions upon which both are ultimately based. The first stage consisted in the long history of the transmission of the old amphictyonic traditions down through the centuries until their formulation into the form of Deuteronomy in the seventh century in Judah. This probably took place during the reign of Manasseh when the circles responsible for it had probably to work underground. When in the reign of Josiah the book was discovered and accepted by the Judaean authorities, the group sprang to life again and began a new phase in the history of their traditions. It was this later phase which eventually led to the composition of the Deuteronomistic history. There is considerable debate as to precisely when this work was compiled, some scholars suggesting that it was a pre-exilic work with post-exilic revision,[1] others arguing that it was composed entirely after the destruction of Jerusalem in 586 B.C. and during the Babylonian exile.[2] Since the last event recorded in this history is the release of Jehoiachin from prison in exile in 561 B.C. (2 Kings xxv. 27f.) without any hint of the return from exile, it seems clear that the *terminus ad quem* for the composition of the work is this same year or slightly later, although it is possible, as we have seen, that these few verses concerning Jehoiachin were an appendix to an already completed work. It is possible, however, that the work had its origins in the late pre-exilic period and was aimed at the twofold task of providing a theological explanation of the destruction and exile of the northern kingdom in 721 B.C. and at the same time inculcating the warnings implicit in this for the southern kingdom which had escaped the destruction wrought upon the north.[3]

If the view of the relationship between the authors of Deuteronomy and the Deuteronomist outlined above is accepted then several relevant points concerning the authorship of Deuteronomy itself emerge. In the first place, it substantiates the theory that the later history of the Deuteronomic circle, the immediate predecessors of the Deuteronomistic party, was centred in Jerusalem. We must now see the Deuteronomic-Deuteronomistic circle as deriving ultimately from northern Israel from whence they fled to Jerusalem after 721 B.C. where they initially drew up their reformation programme in the form of *Urdeuteronomium* and when this was favourably accepted by the Jerusalem authorities continued their activities which culminated in their history work. This also establishes that the interpretation of the centralization law in Deuteronomy as referring to Jerusalem is justified. The same circle who formulated this law clearly believed so.

One further important consideration also emerges. If, as we have argued, there is a direct relationship between the authors of the two works then there is, in the present writer's opinion, some evidence to support the view presented above that the prophetic party was responsible for Deuteronomy. We have seen that the Deuteronomistic history was written in the shadow of the events of 721 B.C. and 586

[1] This is essentially the position of A. Jepsen, *Die Quellen des Königsbuches* (Halle, 1953). Cf. also J. Gray, *I and II Kings* (London, 1964), pp. 13f.

[2] This is the position of Noth, *Überlieferungsgeschichtliche Studien I*^{2} (1957), pp. 91ff.

[3] For the evidence in favour of a pre-exilic compilation of the work and post-exilic revision see J. Gray, op. cit., pp. 13–15.

B.C. and that its central purpose is to provide a theological explanation of why Israel was rejected by Yahweh. It is well known that the answer given to this is that Israel incurred this fate because she had been unfaithful to the will of Yahweh as revealed in the 'law of Moses'. Together with the promulgation of the law had come the stern warning of the curse which would befall the nation in the event of disobedience. Writing as he did after the destruction of the nation, the Deuteronomist saw this curse to have been executed. Von Rad has shown that the realization of this has given rise to one of the most marked characteristics of the Deuteronomist's theology, that is, the belief that Yahweh's word would not 'fail'.[1] Such a belief is expressed in several places in the work (cf. Joshua xxi. 45; xxiii. 14; 1 Kings viii. 56; 2 Kings. x. 10):

> 'Know then that there shall fall to the earth nothing of the word of the Lord, which the Lord spoke. . . .'
>
> (2 Kings x. 10)

But it is most clearly discernible in the prophecy-fulfilment schema which forms one of the basic features of the work and to which von Rad has drawn attention.[2] This scheme consists of a series of prophetic predictions each of which is carefully recorded as having been fulfilled. A few examples from those listed by von Rad will serve to demonstrate this.[3]

Prophecy: In the oracle of Nathan (2 Sam. vii. 12f.) Yahweh promises David that his throne and kingdom will be established by his successors:

> 'When your days are fulfilled and you lie down with your fathers, I will raise up your offspring after you, who shall come forth from your body, and I will establish his kingdom.'

Fulfilment: Solomon becomes king and proclaims (1 Kings viii. 20):

> 'Now the Lord has fulfilled his promise which he made; for I have arisen in the place of David my father, and sit on the throne of Israel, as the Lord promised. . . .'

Prophecy: Ahijah predicts to Jeroboam the division of the Davidic kingdom (1 Kings xi. 30f.):

> 'Then Ahijah laid hold of the new garment that was on him, and tore it into twelve pieces. And he said to Jeroboam, "Take for yourself ten

[1] Cf. G. von Rad, *Studies in Deuteronomy*, pp. 78ff.; idem, *Old Testament Theology*, I, pp. 339f.

[2] G. von Rad, *Studies in Deuteronomy*, pp. 78ff.

[3] Ibid., pp. 78–81.

pieces; for thus says the Lord, the God of Israel, 'Behold, I am about to tear the kingdom from the hand of Solomon, and will give you ten tribes. . . .' " '

Fulfilment: Rehoboam refuses to meet the demands of the people to end the oppressive policies which his father had introduced and the disruption follows (1 Kings xii. 15f.):

> 'So the king did not hearken to the people; for it was a turn of affairs brought about by the Lord that he might fulfil his word, which the Lord spoke by Ahijah the Shilonite to Jeroboam the son of Nebat.'

Prophecy: Ahijah now predicts Jeroboam's own downfall because he had done evil above all that were before him (1 Kings xiv. 7 ff.):

> 'Therefore behold, I will bring evil upon the house of Jeroboam, and will cut off from Jeroboam every male, both bond and free in Israel, and will utterly consume the house of Jeroboam, as a man burns up dung until it is all gone. . . .'

Fulfilment: Jeroboam's successor Nadab is assassinated by Baasha (1 Kings xv. 27f.) who subsequently exterminates the remaining members of Jeroboam's house:

> 'And as soon as he was king, he killed all the house of Jeroboam; he left to the house of Jeroboam not one that breathed, until he had destroyed it, according to the word of the Lord which he spoke by his servant Ahijah the Shilonite.'

Prophecy: Jehu the son of Hanani condemns Baasha for having 'walked in the way of Jeroboam' (1 Kings xvi. 1f.):

> 'And the word of the Lord came to Jehu the son of Hanani against Baasha, saying . . . Behold, I will utterly sweep away Baasha and his house, and I will make your house like the house of Jeroboam the son of Nebat.'

Fulfilment: Zimri assassinates Elah, Baasha's successor, and exterminates his household (1 Kings xvi. 9ff.):

> 'Thus Zimri destroyed all the house of Baasha, according to the word of the Lord, which he spoke against Baasha by Jehu the prophet.'

Prophecy: Elijah prophesies that Ahaziah will not recover from his sickness (2 Kings i. 15–16):

> 'So he arose and went down with him to the king, and said to him, "Thus says the Lord, 'Because you have sent messengers to inquire of

Baal-zebub, the god of Ekron . . . therefore you shall not come down from the bed to which you have gone, but you shall surely die.' " '

Fulfilment: 2 Kings i. 17:

'So he died according to the word of the Lord which Elijah had spoken.

From all this it is clear that the Deuteronomist saw and wished his readers to see a direct relationship between the word of Yahweh as spoken by the prophets and the events of Israel's history.[1] This explains the great amount of prophetic material which the Deuteronomist has used in writing his history. One has only to remember in this connection the space he affords to the Elijah-Elisha sagas as well as his incorporation of some Isaianic material. This interest of the Deuteronomist in the prophetic word as well as the great amount of prophetic material and traditions which he had at his disposal is best understood by seeing him as closely associated with 'old prophecy'.[2] Von Rad indeed has described him as a prophet himself.[3] And is this not of significance in the discussion of the identity of the circle responsible for Deuteronomy? We have seen that there is considerable evidence to show that it was the prophetic party in the northern kingdom who were the custodians of the old amphictyonic traditions underlying the book and that it is to these prophets and their descendants that its authorship is to be attributed. If now it is accepted that the authors of Deuteronomy and the Deuteronomist belonged to one and the same circle of tradition and we are correct in seeing the Deuteronomist party as essentially a prophetic group, then it may be concluded that their Deuteronomic predecessors were likewise prophets. This view would also explain how the Deuteronomist came to be in possession of so much material concerning the activity of the northern prophetic party which occupies so much space in his history. One must presume that all this northern material was brought south by the Deuteronomic circle after 721 B.C. One further consideration substantiates this view of the prophetic nature of the Deuteronomic-Deuteronomistic circle. We saw that in Deuteronomy Moses is conceived of as prophetic covenant mediator responsible for the promulgation and teaching of the law and that he is seen as the first of a series of prophets whom Yahweh would raise up to continue his office (Deut. xviii. 15f.). This in itself would seem to indicate that Deuteronomy regards the prophets as the mediators of the divine law. But that the Deuteronomist believed

[1] Cf. G. von Rad, ibid., p. 81.
[2] Cf. G. von Rad, ibid., p. 83.
[3] G. von Rad. ibid., p. 82.

this to be so is also clear. It is evident in his record of the efforts of the prophets to uphold the law and to demand Israel's obedience to its requirements. But in addition, in at least one place he has explicitly identified the prophets as exercising the functions ascribed by Deuteronomy to Moses:

> 'Yet the Lord warned Israel and Judah by every prophet and every seer, saying "Turn from your evil ways and keep my commandments and my statutes, in accordance with all the law which I commanded your fathers, and which I sent to you by my servants the prophets."'
>
> (2 Kings xvii. 13)

It would seem clear that in this the Deuteronomist, like Deuteronomy itself, is associating the promulgation and teaching of the divine law to Israel with the prophets. What Moses did in Deuteronomy, so also did the prophets during the course of Israel's history.

This brief examination of the work of the Deuteronomist has therefore contributed several important considerations to the discussion of the origin and authorship of Deuteronomy. It supports the view that the immediate background of the work is Jerusalem in the seventh century. At the same time the close association between the authors of Deuteronomy and the Deuteronomist, an association which is best explained by seeing them as belonging to one and the same circle, supports the interpretation of the centralization law in Deuteronomy as referring to Jerusalem. Finally, and perhaps most significant of all, the interest of the Deuteronomist in prophecy and the role which he accords the prophets as the mediators of Yahweh's divine will to Israel supports the view that the Deuteronomic-Deuteronomistic circle was a prophetic circle.

CHAPTER VII

CONCLUSION

THE book of Deuteronomy raises a multiplicity of problems for the student of the Old Testament. In this short study no attempt has been made to cover the many questions involved in the study of the book. What we have been concerned with is the basic problem of the origin of Deuteronomy and the circles responsible for its composition.

The investigation of this vexed problem has been greatly illuminated by new trends and methods developed and applied by Old Testament scholars in recent years as well as by our increasing understanding of the life and institutions of Israel and her ancient near eastern neighbours. In particular, attention has been drawn to the important contribution of the cult to the preservation and transmission of Israel's distinctive traditions and it has become clear that the book of Deuteronomy itself bears striking evidence of liturgical influence. The actual form in which the book is cast follows the pattern of the old Israelite festival of the renewal of the covenant which is now seen to have comprised four basic elements—parenesis and the recollection of Yahweh's saving actions on Israel's behalf in history, the promulgation of the divine laws, a ceremony of covenant making, and the setting forth of blessings and curses—all of which are present in Deuteronomy. In addition, the cult has left its stamp upon the manner in which the book is presented for the marked homiletic style in which it is written points for its origin to a cultic milieu. Such a style must first of all have been developed within a liturgical context before it was employed as a literary style in the Deuteronomic and Deuteronomistic writings. Deuteronomy must therefore be seen as having originated among circles who were at some time in their history closely associated with the cult and who have consequently been strongly influenced by liturgical norms and patterns.

Yet another way in which recent research has contributed towards a better understanding of the provenance of Deuteronomy is the transformation which has come about in our knowledge of the life and institutions of pre-monarchical Israel, the period of the Judges.

Older scholars generally regarded this period as being ultimately of little significance in the development of Israel's distinctive religion. The predominant view of Julius Wellhausen and his contemporaries and associates was that the theological and ethical principles of lasting value in the Old Testament sprang from the teaching of the great canonical prophets. The period before the foundation of the state under the monarchy contributed little or nothing towards this. It was a period lacking in both political and religious unity when 'every man did that which was right in his own eyes'. Today this has been radically changed and the period of the Judges is now regarded as the first great creative period in Israel's history on the soil of Canaan. The researches of Alt and Noth in particular have shown that Israel at this time took on its normative form as a group of twelve tribes in a covenant relationship with Yahweh. It was within the context of the cultic life of this tribal league that Israel's traditions of election and covenant were given their normative form.

The relevance of this for the study of Deuteronomy is, as we have seen, that it is precisely within the traditions which stem from this old Israelite amphictyony that the traditions underlying Deuteronomy had their origin. Various aspects and characteristics of the book point to this. The covenant traditions which it seeks to promulgate are based upon the Sinai covenant which was the basis of the life of the tribes and their relationship with Yahweh. Deuteronomy affords no place to the later covenant traditions centring on Yahweh's choice of David. We also saw how the book is impregnated with the ideology of the old institution of the Holy War which, as von Rad has demonstrated, was one of the basic cultic institutions of early Israel. It was also within the context of the cultic life of the tribal confederation that the covenant renewal festival had its origins and was given its basic form. Here again Deuteronomy shows evidence of its origin within the traditions of the amphictyony.

At the same time it has emerged that Deuteronomy contains no direct deposit of these old sacral traditions of early Israel. There has been considerable development in many ways. Not only do many of the laws within the book point for their origin to a period much in advance of the tribal league, but other old cultic norms such as the Holy War itself have been modified and changed to some extent in Deuteronomy. More important still, we have seen that the book displays evidence of having been influenced to some degree by traditions which originated not in the tribal league but within the context of the specifically Jerusalem cult tradition. This influence is in evidence mainly in the Deuteronomic demand for the centralization of worship to one sanctuary. It was Mount Zion which was believed to stand in a unique relationship with Yahweh and it was in Jerusalem that the first attempt to centralize the cult was carried out. There is no evidence in the Old Testament that any other sanctuary ever claimed the sole monopoly of Israel's worship of Yahweh. Nor is there any indication that anyone other than Hezekiah, and Josiah after him, attempted to abolish the local Yahweh shrines and to limit worship to one place. It is accordingly more scientific to explain the demand for centralization in Deuteronomy as having as its background the claims of the Jerusalem Temple to a position of primacy and, by the time of Hezekiah, to absolute and exclusive cultic centrality than to attempt to explain it as having originated in any other sanctuary, such as Bethel or Shechem, for which there is not a shred of evidence in the Old Testament.

It is clear from all this that we are dealing in Deuteronomy not with an *ad hoc* literary and theological creation of the seventh century B.C. Rather we must see the book as the final product and expression of a long history involving the transmission and constant adaptation of the old traditions of early Israel upon which it is based. The study of Deuteronomy is therefore a study in the history of tradition. The sacral traditions which underlie the book reach back for their origins into the amphictyonic period and indeed further back into the pre-conquest period to the events at Sinai which marked the sequel to the election of Israel by Yahweh in the exodus and the beginning of her relationship with him in terms of covenant. Deuteronomy can therefore be said to be the deposit of the authentic Mosaic faith as it developed during the course of Israel's history in the land of Canaan. This stream of tradition was transmitted down through the centuries until in the seventh century and under the shadow of the destruction of the northern tribes and the threat of a similar fate for the remaining Judaean kingdom it was formulated into the book of Deuteronomy in an attempt to revive the nation and ensure its future as Yahweh's covenant people.

When we inquire into the question of where these traditions had their home during the course of their history and transmission, the evidence in the Old Testament points to northern Israel. It was in the north that the amphictyony had had its centre at the old sanctuaries of Shechem, Bethel, Gilgal and Shiloh. At these places the traditions were cultically transmitted for a considerable period of Israel's history beginning in the period of the tribal league and continuing down through the early years of the monarchy perhaps even up to the late ninth century. It was not until the time of David that they moved to Jerusalem. But here there developed another tradition based upon the belief in a unique covenant relationship between Yahweh and the house of David. This later covenant tradition represented a far-reaching development of the older Sinai traditions which were eventually subordinated to it and fell into a secondary place in the specifically Jerusalem cult tradition. But in the north they were preserved tenaciously down through the period of the monarchy.

As to the circles responsible for the preservation and transmission of the traditions underlying Deuteronomy, we have seen that there is an abundance of evidence in the Old Testament to suggest that it is primarily the prophetic circles in northern Israel to whom we are to look. Beginning with Samuel there arose a series of prophetic personalities and groups who cherished the old traditions from generation to generation. It was this prophetic circle who were the custodians and preservers of the traditions during such periods as that which forms the background to the preaching of Hosea and Amos when the cultic transmission of the covenant faith seems to have collapsed. There is little evidence in the Old Testament to suggest that levites were the bearers of the traditions underlying Deuteronomy. The suggestions of von Rad and Wolff which advance such a view find little or no concrete evidence to support them in the Old Testament documents. If, as they argue, the levites were responsible for Deuteronomy then it is astonishing that no record has been left of their activity in the Deuteronomic and Deuteronomistic writings. Here, as we have seen, the role of the prophet as covenant mediator is repeatedly recorded. In Deuteronomy itself Moses is portrayed as prophet and not priest and he is seen as the first of a series of prophetic personalities whom Yahweh promises to raise up to continue his office.

It may be concluded therefore that the book of Deuteronomy originated among circles of prophets who were active in northern Israel. But it emerged during our discussion that the book played some part in the reformation carried out by Josiah in Judah in the late seventh century and this raised the question of how such a northern stream of tradition found its way in the form of Deuteronomy into the Jerusalem Temple at this time. We saw that the most plausible solution to this was that the circles among whom it originated, though deriving from northern Israel, fled south to Judah after the collapse and destruction of the northern kingdom in 721 B.C. Here they continued their work in the belief that the future of Israel as Yahweh's covenant people lay with the southern people who had remained relatively untouched by the devastation wrought by the Assyrians upon their northern brethren. It soon became apparent to the Deuteronomic circle that the Judaean authorities were intent upon reviving the nation. The first opportunity for doing so came in Hezekiah's reign when the Assyrian power was momentarily weakened by domestic disturbances. But the attempt was short-lived and when Assyria regained control the policy was abandoned. During the subsequent reign of Manasseh reaction set in against Hezekiah's cultic reforms and there seems to have been a renewal of idolatry perhaps on a worse scale than before. It was at this time that the Deuteronomic circle drew up their own programme of reform and revival. In doing so they embodied some of the lessons of Hezekiah's abortive reformation attempt. They centred their plans for renewal in Jerusalem and accorded its claims to cultic primacy the authority of the 'law of Moses'. Their book was then deposited at some time in the Temple in Jerusalem and when Josiah came to the throne and there arose once more the opportunity for reform and revival it was discovered and accepted by the Judaean authorities as the will of Yahweh for his people. As a result of this, the older Sinai covenant tradition which had been overshadowed by the Davidic covenant tradition in the Jerusalem cult rose once again to a position of priority.

When Deuteronomy was thus accorded a place within the reformation activity of the Judaean authorities, the Deuteronomic circle once more sprang to life. This, as we have suggested, inaugurated a new phase in the history of the circle and culminated in the great Deuteronomistic history work contained in the corpus Deuteronomy–2 Kings. There is some evidence that this work may already have been begun in the late pre-exilic period. But in its present form it was composed some time after the downfall and exile of Judah in 586 B.C. and perhaps before but certainly not much later than 561 B.C. when Jehoiachin was released from prison in exile (2 Kings xxv. 27f.).

The Deuteronomic-Deuteronomistic literature is thus the final expression of a long history of the faithful preservation and transmission of Israel's normative covenant faith. This history is the record of the continual conflict of those who cherished that faith with anything or anyone who threatened its existence. When finally they formulated their traditions into the book of Deuteronomy once more they were striving to keep that faith alive in the face of tremendous odds. When this bold attempt to gather together their people and recall them to the service of their God failed and Yahweh's judgment fell upon Israel, they saw it as the wrath of a righteous God upon a wayward and disobedient people. Yahweh's word had been fulfilled; the curse which the gift of the covenant had embodied from the beginning had fallen upon Israel. Yet even here hope was not abandoned. The Deuteronomistic history was no mere academic exercise. Nor was it intended solely as further rebuke to those who had suffered Yahweh's rejection, for in seeking to show how this had come about it was holding forth the hope that even now the broken relationship with God could be healed if only Israel returned to him in penitence.

LIST OF ABBREVIATIONS

ATD	*Das Alte Testament Deutsch*
BA	*The Biblical Archaeologist*
BKAT	*Biblischer Kommentar: Altes Testament*
BJRL	*Bulletin of the John Rylands Library*
BWAT	*Beiträge zur Wissenschaft vom Alten Testament*
BWANT	*Beiträge zur Wissenschaft vom Alten und Neuen Testament*
BZAW	*Beihefte zur Zeitschrift für die alttestamentliche Wissenschaft*
CAH	*Cambridge Ancient History*, ed. J. B. Bury, S. A. Cook, F. E. Adcock, Cambridge, 1923–39
CBSC	*The Cambridge Bible for Schools and Colleges*
ExpT	*Expository Times*
EvTh	*Evangelische Theologie*
FRLANT	*Forschungen zur Religion und Literatur des Alten und Neuen Testaments*
HDB	*Hasting's Dictionary of the Bible*
IB	*The Interpreter's Bible*
ICC	*The International Critical Commentary*
IDB	*The Interpreter's Dictionary of the Bible*, New York-Nashville, 1962
IEJ	*Israel Exploration Journal*
JBL	*Journal of Biblical Literature*
JNES	*Journal of Near Eastern Studies*
JQR	*Jewish Quarterly Review*
JR	*Journal of Religion*
JSS	*Journal of Semitic Studies*
JTS	*Journal of Theological Studies*
LXX	The Septuagint
MT	The Massoretic Text
OLZ	*Orientalistische Literaturzeitung*
OTMS	*The Old Testament and Modern Study*, ed. H. H. Rowley, Oxford, 1951
PEQ	*Palestine Exploration Quarterly*
RHR	*Revue de l'Histoire des Religions*
TGUOS	*Transactions of the Glasgow University Oriental Society*
TLZ	*Theologische Literaturzeitung*
ThWzNT	*Theologisches Wörterbuch zum Neuen Testament*
VT	*Vetus Testamentum*
ZA	*Zeitschrift für Assyriologie*
ZAW	*Zeitschrift für die alttestamentliche Wissenschaft*
ZDMG	*Zeitschrift der Deutschen Morgenländischen Gesellschaft*

BIBLIOGRAPHY

ADDIS, W. E., *The Documents of the Hexateuch*, I, London, 1892, II, 1898.
ALBRIGHT, W. F., *From the Stone Age to Christianity*[2], Baltimore, 1946.
ALT, A., 'Die Wallfahrt von Sichem nach Bethel', *Kleine Schriften*, I, Munich, 1953, pp. 79–88.
'Die Ursprünge des israelitischen Rechts', *Kleine Schriften*, I, 1953, pp. 278–332.
'Die Staatenbildung der Israeliten in Palästina', *Kleine Schriften*, II, 1953, pp. 1–65.
'Das Königtum in den Reichen Israel und Juda', *Kleine Schriften*, II, 1953, pp. 116–134.
'Die Heimat des Deuteronomiums', *Kleine Schriften*, II, 1953, pp. 250–275.
'Judas Gaue unter Josia', *Kleine Schriften*, II, 1953, pp. 276–288.
AMSLER, S., *David, Roi et Messie. La tradition davidique dans l'Ancien Testament* (Cahiers theologique 49), Neuchâtel, 1963.
ANDERSON, B. W., *The Living World of the Old Testament*, London, 1958.
ANDERSON, G. W., *A Critical Introduction to the Old Testament*, London, 1959.
BÄCHLI, O., *Israel und die Völker. Eine Studie zum Deuteronomium*, Zürich, 1962.
BENTZEN, A., *Die josianische Reform und ihre Voraussetzungen*, Copenhagen, 1926.
Introduction to the Old Testament[4], Copenhagen, 1958.
BERRY, G. R., 'The Code found in the Temple', *JBL* 39, 1920, pp. 44–51.
'The Date of Deuteronomy', *JBL* 59, 1940, pp. 133–139.
BERTHOLET, A., *Das Deuteronomium*, Leipzig, 1899.
BEWER, J. A. *The Literature of the Old Testament*,[3] revised by E. J. Kraeling, New York and London, 1962.
'A Symposium on the Problem of Deuteronomy', *JBL* 47, 1928, pp. 305–379 (with G. Dahl and L. B. Paton).
BEYERLIN, W. *Die Kulttraditionen Israels in der Verkündigung des Propheten Micha* (*FRLANT* 72), Göttingen, 1959.
Origins and History of the Oldest Sinaitic Traditions, Oxford, 1965.
BOWMAN, J., 'The Samaritans and the Book of Deuteronomy', *TGUOS* 17, 1958, pp. 9–18.
BREIT, H., *Die Predigt des Deuteronomisten*, Munich, 1933.
BRIGHT, J., *A History of Israel*, London, 1960.
Early Israel in Recent History Writing, London, 1956.
Joshua, *Interpreter's Bible*, II, New York-Nashville, 1953.
BRINKER, R., *The Influence of Sanctuaries in Early Israel*, Manchester, 1946.
BUDDE, K., 'Das Deuteronomium und die Reform Josias', *ZAW* 44, 1926, pp. 177–224.
BURKITT, F. C., A review of Kennett's *Deuteronomy and the Decalogue* in *JTS* 22, 1921, pp. 61–65.
A note in *JBL* 40, 1921, p. 167.
BURNEY, C. F., *The Book of Judges*, London, 1918.
CAMPBELL, E. F., 'Excavation at Shechem 1960', *BA* vol. 23 no. 4, 1960.

'The Excavation of Shechem and the Biblical Tradition', *BA* vol. 26, no. 1, 1963 (with J. F. Ross).
CARPENTER, J. E., *The Composition of the Hexateuch*, London, 1902 (with G. Harford).
CAZELLES, H., *Etudes sur le Code de L'Alliance*, Paris, 1946.
Introduction à la Bible, Paris, 1953.
Le Deutéronome, Paris, 1958.
CLEMENTS, R. E., 'Temple and Land: a Significant Aspect of Israel's Worship', *TGUOS* 19, 1963, pp. 16–28.
Prophecy and Covenant, London, 1965.
God and Temple, Oxford, 1965.
'Deuteronomy and the Jerusalem Cult Tradition', *VT* 15, 1965, pp. 300–312.
COOK, S. A., *Cambridge Ancient History*, vol. III, 1925, pp. 406f., 481ff.
CORNILL, C. H., *Einleitung in das Alte Testament*, Leipzig, 1891.
Introduction to the Canonical Books of the Old Testament, London 1907.
CROSS, F. M., 'Josiah's Revolt against Assyria', *JNES* 12, 1953, pp. 56–58 (with D. N. Freedman).
'The Boundary Lists of the Kingdom of Judah', *JBL* 75, 1956, pp. 202–226 (with G. E. Wright).
CULLEN, J., *The Book of the Covenant in Moab*, Glasgow, 1903.
DAICHES, S., 'The meaning of am ha-aretz in the Old Testament', *JTS* 30, 1929, pp. 245–249.
DANNELL, G.A., *Studies in the Name Israel in the Old Testament*, Uppsala, 1946.
DAVIES, G. HENTON, 'Deuteronomy' in *Peake's Commentary*², London, 1962.
DAY, E., 'The Promulgation of Deuteronomy', *JBL* 21, 1902, pp. 197–213.
DORNSEIFF, F., 'Antikes zum Alten Testament: 4. Die Abfassungszeit des Pentateuch und die Deuteronomiumsfrage', *ZAW* 56, 1938, pp. 64–85.
DRIVER, G. R., 'Notes and Studies', *JTS* 39, 1938, pp. 154ff.
DRIVER, S. R., *Deuteronomy*³, *ICC*, Edinburgh, 1902.
Exodus, *CBSC*, Cambridge, 1918.
*Introduction to the Literature of the Old Testament*⁹, Edinburgh, 1913.
DUBBERSTEIN, W. H., 'Assyrian-Babylonian Chronology', *JNES* 3, 1944, pp. 38–46.
DUMERMUTH, F., 'Zur deuteronomischen Kulttheologie und ihre Voraussetzungen', *ZAW* 70, 1958, pp. 59–98.
EERDMANS, B. D., 'Deuteronomy' in *Old Testament Essays*, ed. D. C. Simpson, London, 1927, pp. 77–84.
EICHRODT, W., *Theology of the Old Testament*, I, London, 1961.
EISSFELDT, O., *The Old Testament: An Introduction*, Oxford, 1965.
'Lade und Stierbild', *ZAW* 58, 1940–41, pp. 190–215, now in his *Kleine Schriften*, II, Tübingen, 1963, pp. 282–305.
ELMSLIE, W. A. L. *Chronicles*, *Interpreter's Bible*, III, New York-Nashville, 1954.
ENGNELL, I., *Symbolae Biblicae Uppsalienses*, 7, 1946, pp. 21f.
FREED, A., 'The Code spoken of in II Kings xxii–xxiii', *JBL* 40, 1921, pp. 76–80.

FREEDMAN, D. N. See under Cross, F. M.
GEHMAN, H. S., See under Montgomery, J. A.
GILLISCHEWSKI, E., 'Der Ausdruck Am Ha-arez im A.T.', *ZAW* 40, 1922, pp. 137–142.
GORDIS, R., 'Sectional Rivalry in the Kingdom of Judah', *JQR* 25, 1934–35, pp. 237–259.
GORDON, C., *Before the Bible*, London, 1962.
GRAHAM, W. E., 'The Modern Controversy about Deuteronomy', *JR* 7, 1927, pp. 396–418.
GRAY, J., *I and II Kings*, London, 1964.
GRESSMANN, H., 'Josia and das Deuteronomium', *ZAW* 42, 1924, pp. 313–337.
HALDAR, A., *Associations of Cult Prophets among the Ancient Semites*, Uppsala, 1945.
HARFORD, G., See under Carpenter, J. E.
HEMPEL, J., *Die Schichten des Deuteronomiums*, Leipzig, 1914.
Die Althebräische Literatur, Wildpark-Potsdam, 1930–34.
HERBERT, A. S., 'I and II Chronicles' in *Peake's Commentary*², London, 1962.
HÖLSCHER, G., 'Komposition und Ursprung des Deuteronomiums', *ZAW* 40, 1922, pp. 161–255.
Geschichte der israelitischen und jüdischen Religion, Giessen, 1922.
'Das Buch der Könige: seine Quellen und seine Redaktion', in *Eucharisterion für Gunkel, FRLANT* 18, 1923, pp. 158–213.
HORST, F., 'Die Kultusreform des Königs Josia', *ZDMG* 77, 1923, pp. 220–238.
'Die Anfänge des Propheten Jeremia', *ZAW* 41, 1923, pp. 94–153.
'Das Privilegrecht Jahwes', *FRLANT* 45, 1930, now in his *Gesammelte Studien*, Munich, 1961, pp. 17–154.
JEPSEN, A., *Die Quellen des Königsbuches*, Halle, 1953.
'Die Reform des Josias' in *Baumgärtel Festschrift*, ed. J. Herrmann, Erlangen, 1959.
JOHNSON, A. R., 'The Prophet in Israelite Worship', *ExpT* 47, 1935–36, pp. 312ff.
Sacral Kingship in Ancient Israel, Cardiff, 1955.
*The Cultic Prophet in Ancient Israel*², Cardiff, 1962.
JUNGE, E., *Der Wiederaufbau des Heerwesens des Reiches Juda unter Josia, BWANT* IV:23, Stuttgart, 1937.
JUNKER, H., 'Die Entstehungszeit des Ps. 78 und das Deuteronomium', *Biblica* 34, 1953, pp. 487–500.
KENNEDY, A. R. S., 'Golden Calf' in *HDB*, vol. I, Edinburgh, 1898, pp. 340f.
KENNETT, R. H., 'The Origin of the Aaronite Priesthood', *JTS* 6, 1905, pp. 161–186.
'The Date of Deuteronomy', *JTS* 7, 1906, pp. 481–500.
Deuteronomy and the Decalogue, Cambridge, 1920.
KJAER, H., 'The Danish Excavation of Shiloh', *PEQ* 59, 1927, pp. 202–213.
KOCH, K., 'Zur Geschichte der Erwählungsvorstellung in Israel', *ZAW* 67, 1955, pp. 205–226.
KÖNIG, E., *Das Deuteronomium*, Leipzig, 1917.

'Stimmen Exod. xx. 24 und Deut. xii. 13f. zusammen?', *ZAW* 42, 1924, pp. 337–346.
'Der generelle Artikel im Hebräischen', *ZAW* 44, 1926, pp. 173f.
KRAUS, H.-J. *Die Königsherrschaft Gottes im Alten Testament*, Tübingen, 1951.
Worship in Israel, Oxford, 1966.
'Zur Geschichte des Passah-Massot-Festes im Alten Testament', *EvTh* 18, 1958, pp. 44–67.
LINDBLOM, J., *Prophecy in Ancient Israel*, Oxford, 1962.
LOISY, A., *Religion d'Israel*[3], Paris, 1933.
MAAG, V., 'Erwägungen zur deuteronomischen Kultzentralisation', *VT* 6, 1956, pp. 10–18.
MALAMAT, A., 'The Historical Background to the Assassination of Amon King of Judah', *IEJ* 3, 1953, pp. 26–29.
MANLEY, G. T., *The Book of the Law: Studies in the Date of Deuteronomy*, London, 1957.
McKANE, W., *I and II Samuel*, London, 1963.
McKENZIE, J. L., 'Knowledge of God in Hosea', *JBL* 74, 1955, pp. 22f.
MAUCHLINE, J., *Hosea*, *Interpreter's Bible*, VI, New York-Nashville, 1956.
'I and II Kings' in *Peake's Commentary*[2], London, 1962.
MENDENHALL, G. E., 'Covenant Forms in Israelite Tradition', *BA* 17, no. 3, 1954.
'Election', *IDB* II, pp. 76–82.
MITCHELL, H. G., 'The Use of the Second Person in Deuteronomy', *JBL* 18, 1899, pp. 61–109.
MONTGOMERY, J. A., *Kings*, *ICC*, Edinburgh, 1951 (with H. S. Gehman).
MORAN, W. L., Review of O. Bächli's *Israel und die Völker* in *Biblica* 44, 1963, pp. 375–377.
MOWINCKEL, S., *Psalmenstudien I–VI*, rep. Amsterdam, 1961.
Le Décalogue, Paris, 1927.
The Psalms in Israel's Worship, I and II, Oxford, 1962.
MUILENBURG, J., 'The form and structure of the covenantal formulations', *VT* 9, 1959, pp. 347–365.
NEWMAN, M. L., 'The Prophetic Call of Samuel', *Israel's Prophetic Heritage*, ed. B. W. Anderson and W. Harrelson, London, 1962.
The People of the Covenant, New York-Nashville, 1962.
NESTLE, E., 'Das Deuteronomium und II Könige xxii', *ZAW* 22, 1902, pp. 170f., 312f.
NICHOLSON, E. W., 'II Kings xxii. 18—A Simple Restoration', *Hermathena* 97, 1963, pp. 96–98.
'The Centralization of the Cult in Deuteronomy', *VT* 13, 1963, pp. 380–389.
'The Meaning of the Expression עם הארץ in the Old Testament', *JSS* 10, 1965, pp. 59–66.
'Josiah's Reformation and Deuteronomy', *TGUOS* 20, 1965, pp. 77–84.
NIELSEN, E., *Oral Tradition*, London, 1954.
Shechem: a Traditio-historical Investigation[2], Copenhagen, 1959.
NORTH, C. R., 'Pentateuchal Criticism', *OTMS*, ed. H. H. Rowley, Oxford, 1951.

NOTH, M., *Das System der zwölf Stämme Israels*, *BWANT* IV: 1, Stuttgart, 1930.
Überlieferungsgeschichte des Pentateuch, Stuttgart, 1948.
*Überlieferungsgeschichtliche Studien I*², Tübingen, 1957.
'Das Amt des "Richters Israels" ' in *Bertholet Festschrift*, Tübingen, 1950, pp. 404–417.
'Die Gesetze im Pentateuch', *Gesammelte Studien*, Munich, 1960, pp. 9–141.
'Jerusalem und die israelitische Tradition', *Gesammelte Studien*, pp. 172–187.
*The History of Israel*², London, 1960.
Exodus, London, 1962.
NYBERG, H. S., *Studien zum Hoseabuche*, Uppsala, 1935.
OBBINK, K. T., 'Jahwebilder', *ZAW* 47, 1929, pp. 264–274.
OESTERLEY, W. O. E., *Introduction to the Books of the Old Testament*, London, 1934 (with T. H. Robinson).
OESTREICHER, TH., *Das Deuteronomische Grundgesetz*, Gütersloh, 1923.
'Dtn. xii 13f. im Licht von Dtn. xxiii 16f.', *ZAW* 43, 1925, pp. 246–249.
OPPENHEIM, A. L., 'Assyria', *IDB*, I, pp. 262–304.
PATON, L. B., See above under Bewer, J. A.
PEDERSEN, JOHS., *Israel: Its Life and Culture III–IV*, Copenhagen, 1940.
'Passahfest und Passahlegende', *ZAW* 52, 1934, pp. 161ff.
PFEIFFER, R. H., *Introduction to the Old Testament*, New York, 1948.
POPE, M. H., 'Amha-arez', *IDB*, I, pp. 106f.
PORTEOUS, N. W., 'The Prophets and the Problem of Continuity', *Israel's Prophetic Heritage*, ed. B. W. Anderson and G. Harrelson, London, 1962, pp. 11–25.
'Actualization and the Prophetic Criticism of the Cult', *Tradition und Situation. Studien zur alttestamentlichen Prophetie*, Festschrift für A. Weiser, ed. E. Würthwein and O. Kaiser, Göttingen, 1963, pp. 93–105.
PUUKKO, A. F., *Das Deuteronomium*, Leipzig, 1910.
QUELL, G., 'Die Erwählung im A.T.', *ThWzNT* IV (1942).
VON RAD, G., 'Das Gottesvolk im Deuteronomium', *BWANT* III: 2, Stuttgart, 1929.
'Das formgeschichtliche Problem des Hexateuch', *Gesammelte Studien*, Munich, 1958, pp. 9–86.
Studies in Deuteronomy, London, 1953.
Der Heilige Krieg im alten Israel, Göttingen, 1958.
Old Testament Theology, I, London, 1962.
'Deuteronomy', *IDB*, I, pp. 831–838.
Deuteronomium, *ATD*, Göttingen, 1964.
REIDER, J., *Deuteronomy*, London, 1937.
RINGGREN, H., *The Faith of the Psalmists*, London, 1963.
Israelitische Religion, Stuttgart, 1963.
ROBERTSON, E., *The Old Testament Problem*, Manchester, 1950.
ROBINSON, T. H. See under Oesterley, W.O.E.
ROSS, J. F., See under Campbell, E. F.
ROWLEY, H. H., *The Growth of the Old Testament*, London, 1950.
'The Prophet Jeremiah and the Book of Deuteronomy', now in his *From Moses to Qumran*, London, 1963, pp. 187–208.

'Hezekiah's Reform and Rebellion', now in his *Men of God*, London, 1963, pp. 98–132.
'The Early Prophecies of Jeremiah', *Men of God*, pp. 133–168.
RUDOLPH, W., *Chronikbücher*, Tübingen, 1955.
SAGGS, H. W. F., *The Greatness that was Babylon*, London, 1962.
SCHOFIELD, J. N., 'The Significance of the Prophets for the Dating of Deuteronomy', *Studies in History and Religion*, ed. A. E. Payne, London, 1942, pp. 44–60.
' "All Israel" in the Deuteronomic Writers', *Essays and Studies Presented to S. A. Cook*, ed. D. Winton Thomas, London, 1950, pp. 25–34.
SEGAL, M. H., 'The Composition of the Pentateuch—a fresh examination', *Scripta Hierosolymitana*, VIII, Jerusalem, 1961, pp. 68–114.
SELLIN, E., *Introduction to the Old Testament*, London, 1923.
Einleitung in das Alte Testament[8], ed. by L. Rost, Heidelberg, 1950.
SIEBENS, A. R., *L'Origine du Code Deutéronomique*, Paris, 1929.
SLOUSH, N., 'Representative Government among the Hebrews and Phoenicians', *JQR* 4, 1913, pp. 303–310.
SMITH, G. A., *Deuteronomy*, *CBSC*, Cambridge, 1918.
SPERBER, J., 'Der Personenwechsel in der Bibel', *ZA* 30, 1918, pp. 23–33.
STAERK, W., *Das Deuteronomium: sein Inhalt und seine literarische Form*, Leipzig, 1894.
Das Problem des Deuteronomiums, Gütersloh, 1924.
STEUERNAGEL, K., *Der Rahmen des Deuteronomiums*, Halle, 1894.
Die Entstehung des deuteronomischen Gesetz, 1895.
STALKER, D. M. G., 'Exodus' in *Peake's Commentary*[2], London, 1962.
SULZBERGER, M., *The Am Ha-aretz: the ancient Hebrew Parliament*, Philadelphia, 1909.
'The Polity of the Ancient Hebrews', *JQR* 3, 1912–13, pp. 1–81.
DE TILLESSE, G. MINETTE, 'Sections "tu" et sections "vous" dans le Deutéronome', *VT* 12, 1962, pp. 29–87.
DE VAUX, R., *Ancient Israel*, London, 1961.
VRIEZEN, TH. C., *Die Erwählung Israels nach dem Alten Testament*, Zürich, 1953.
An Outline of Old Testament Theology, Oxford, 1958.
WEISER, A., *Introduction to the Old Testament*, London, 1961.
Das Buch der zwölf kleinen Propheten, I, *ATD*, Göttingen, 1949.
The Psalms, London, 1962.
WELCH, A. C., *The Code of Deuteronomy: a new theory of its origin*, London, 1924.
'The two descriptions of the sanctuary in Deuteronomy', *ExpT* 36, 1924–25, pp. 442–444.
'When was the worship of Israel centralized at the Temple?', *ZAW* 43, 1925, pp. 250–255.
'The two descriptions of the sanctuary in Deuteronomy', *ExpT* 37, 1925–26, pp. 215–219.
'On the method of celebrating Passover', *ZAW* 45, 1927, pp. 24–29.
'The Problem of Deuteronomy', *JBL* 43, 1929, pp. 291–306.
Deuteronomy: the framework to the code, London, 1932.
WELLHAUSEN, J., *Prolegomena to the History of Israel*, Edinburgh, 1895.
Die Composition des Hexateuchs, Berlin, 1899.

DE WETTE, W. M. L., *Beiträge zur Einleitung in das A.T.*, I, Berlin, 1806.
WOLFF, H. W., 'Hoseas geistige Heimat', *Gesammelte Studien*, Munich, 1964, pp. 232–250.
' "Wissen um Gott" bei Hosea als Urform von Theologie', *Gesammelte Studien*, pp. 182–205.
Hosea, *BKAT*, Neukirchen, 1961.
WRIGHT, G. E., *The Old Testament against its Environment*, London, 1950.
God who Acts, London, 1952.
Deuteronomy, *Interpreter's Bible*, II, 1953.
*Biblical Archaeology*², London, 1962.
'Cult and History', *Interpretation* 16, 1962, pp. 3–20.
See also under Cross, F.M.
WÜRTHWEIN, E., *Der 'am ha 'arez im Alten Testament*, *BWANT* IV:17, Stuttgart, 1936.
YOUNG, E. J., *An Introduction to the Old Testament*, revised edit., London, 1964.

BIBLICAL REFERENCES

INDEX OF AUTHORS

GENERAL INDEX